FLORENCE

KNOPF CITYMAP GUIDES

Welcome to Florence!

This opening fold-out contains a general map of Florence to help you visualize the 6 large districts discussed in this guide, and 4 pages of valuable information, handy tips and useful addresses.

Discover Florence through 6 districts and 6 maps

A Centro Storico
B Santa Maria Novella
C San Lorenzo
D Santa Croce
E Santo Spirito / San Frediano
F San Miniato al Monte

For each district there is a double-page of addresses (restaurants – listed in ascending order of price – pubs, bars, music venues and stores) followed by a fold-out map for the relevant area with the essential places to see (indicated on the map by a star ★). These places are by no means all that Florence has to offer but to us they are unmissable. The grid-referencing system (**A** B2) makes it easy for you to pinpoint addresses quickly on the map.

Transport and hotels in Florence

The last fold-out consists of a transport map and 4 pages of practical information that include a selection of hotels.

Thematic index

Lists all the sites and addresses featured in this guide.

Welcome to Florence!

A Centro Storico
B Santa Maria Novella
C San Lorenzo

D Santa Croce
E Santo Spirito / San Frediano
F San Miniato al Monte

TORRENTE MUGNONE

VIALE FRANCESCO REDI

SAN JACOPINO

VIA PIETRO TOSELLI

VIA DEL PONTE ALLE MOSSE

Piazza San Jacopino

VIA B. MARCELLO

VIALE F.

CANALE MACINANTE

V. LE F.

IPPODROMO DELLE CASCINE

STAZIONE F.S. PORTA AL PRATO

VIALE BELFIORE

VIALE F.LLI ROSSELLI

LE CASCINE

V. LE

PORTA AL PRATO

Piazza Vittorio Veneto

STAZIONE CENTRALE F.S. SANTA MARIA NOVELLA

FIUME

ARNO

TEATRO COMUNALE

S. MARIA NOVELLA

VIA DEL SANSOVINO

VIA DE' VANNI

Piazza T. Gaddi

OGNISSANTI

VIA A. DEL POLLAIOLO

VIA BRONZINO

PIGNONE

Piazza d'Ognissanti

Piazza di Cestello

VILLA STROZZI

Piazza Pier Vettori

Piazza d'Ognissanti

B

V.LE A. ALEARDI

SAN FREDIANO IN CESTELLO

MONTICELLI

SAN FREDIANO

SANTO SPIRITO

VILLA MONTE ULIVETO

Piazza T. Tasso

S. MARIA D. CARMINE

VILLA FIORAVANTI

SANTO SPIRITO

Piazza S. Francesco di Paola

VIALE F. PETRARCA

GIARDINO TORRIGIANI

MUSEO ZOOLOGICO LA SPECOLA

PORTA ROMANA

Piazzale di Porta Romana

E

ISTITUTO D'ARTE

VIALE DEL POGGIO IMPERIALE

V. LE N.

VIA SENESE

(550 yards)
0   250   500m
1/25 000 - 1cm = 250 m

SAN GAGGIO

San Lorenzo

C

An entire district sprang up as a result of the impetus given by the first Medici, Cosimo Il Vecchio (the Elder), and then by Lorenzo the Magnificent – look for their impressive palace, their library, and the church of San Lorenzo, one of Florence's most precious treasures. Further north is the university district, and the flow of students passing through Piazza San Marco makes it one of the liveliest squares in the city. It is bordered by two major monuments: the convent of San Marco, which boasts some of Fra Angelico's most mystical work, and the Academy of Fine Arts. Many Florentines live in northeast Florence, which is why so many authentic groceries and restaurants are here.

MERCATO CENTRALE

ZÀ-ZÀ

RESTAURANTS

Mercato Centrale (C A4)
➔ *Piazza di Mercato Centrale. Mon-Sat 7am–2pm (4–7pm Sat, winter)*
Surrounded by the leather market, this beautiful 19th-century covered market is a riot of colors, fragrances and flavors. This is the perfect place for lunch: visit Nerbone to see proprietors and laborers enjoying tripe at the same table (5 €); or go to Perini to sample the grocer's *crostini* and put together a mouthwatering picnic.

Il Vegetariano (C B2)
➔ *Via delle Ruote, 3or*
Tel. 055 47 50 30
Daily 12.30–3pm, 7.30pm–midnight. Closed Sat, Sun lunch and Mon
One of Florence's few vegetarian restaurants, with a shady arbor for eating al fresco in the summer and a cozy interior in the winter. Zucchini and mushroom risotto, eggplant gratin, chocolate cake, crumble, cheesecake. Dishes 6 €.

Zà-Zà (C A4)
➔ *Piazza di Mercato Centrale, 26 r*
Tel. 055 21 54 11
Mon-Sat lunch and dinner
This delightful restaurant is always packed. In summer, diners sit on the terrace overlooking the market. Soups, *tagliata al tartufo* (minced beef in a truffle sauce on a bed of rocket) and apple puffs. Dishes 10 €.

Lo Skipper (C C4)
➔ *Via degli Alfani, 78a/r*
Tel. 055 28 40 19.
Daily 10am–midnight.
Closed Sat lunch and Sun
This is the sailing club restaurant, tucked away to the right of the Opificio delle Pietre Dure. The Neapolitan chef and owner lovingly prepares Tuscan dishes with an exotic twist. Every month he celebrates the flavors of a particular region or country: Greece, Mexico, Sicily. Booking essential. Dishes 8 –10 €.

Le Tre Panche (C F1)
➔ *Via A. Pacinotti, 32r*
Tel. 055 583 724
Mon-Sat noon–3pm, 8pm–midnight
As its name suggests, this restaurant has just three benches. Delicious wine by the carafe, authentic risotto and pasta dishes. Dishes 10 €.

Perseus (C D1)
➔ *Viale Don G. Minzoni, 1or. Tel. 055 58 82 26*
Mon-Sat noon–2.30pm, 7.30–11pm

San Lorenzo

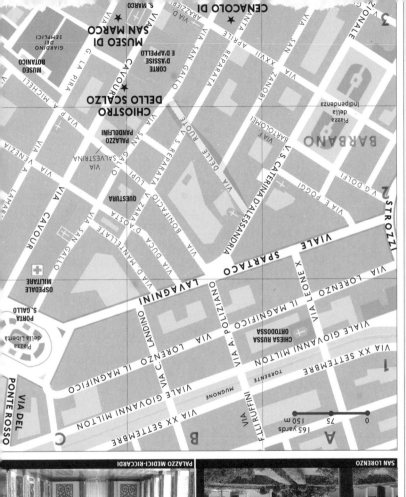

CENACOLO DI
S. MARCO

MUSEO DI
SAN MARCO

GIARDINO
DEI
SEMPLICI

MUSEO
BOTANICO

CORTE
D'ASSISE
E D'APPELLO

CHIOSTRO
DELLO SCALZO

PALAZZO
PANDOLFINI

QUESTURA

Piazza
della
Indipendenza

BARBANO

OSPEDALE
MILITARE

PORTA
S. GALLO

Piazza
della Libertà

CHIESA RUSSA
ORTODOSSA

VIA DEL
PONTE ROSSO

VIALE SPARTACO LAVAGNINI

VIA CAVOUR

VIA SAN GALLO

VIA S. REPARATA

VIA DELLE RUOTE

VIA V.S. CATERINA D'ALESSANDRIA

VIALE E. POGGI

VIA G. DOLFI

V. STROZZI

VIA SAN ZANOBI

VIA XXVII APRILE

VIA S. REPARATA

VIA SAN GALLO

VIA V. ZARA

VIA DUCA D'AOSTA

VIA DELLE RUOTE

VIA SALVESTRINA

VIA BONIFACIO LUPI

VIA MANTELLATE

VIA C. LANDINO

VIALE GIOVANNI MILTON

VIA LORENZO IL MAGNIFICO

VIA A. POLIZIANO

VIA LORENZO IL MAGNIFICO

VIA LEONE X

VIALE GIOVANNI MILTON

VIA XX SETTEMBRE

VIA XX SETTEMBRE

VIA F.LLI RUFFINI

MUGNONE

TORRENTE

VIA P. A. MICHELI

VIA G. LA PIRA

VIA P. A. MICHELI

VIA VENEZIA

VIA LAMARMORA

0   75   150 m

165 yards

SAN LORENZO

PALAZZO MEDICI-RICCARDI

SANTA
APOLLONIA

Piazza
S. Marco

UNIVERSITÀ

BIBLIOTECA
MARUCELLIANA

SANTISSIMA
ANNUNZIATA

★
GALLERIA
DELL'ACCADEMIA

MERCATO
CENTRALE

Piazza d.
Mercato
Centrale

PIAZZA DELLA ★
SS. ANNUNZIATA

M
ARCHE

OPIFICIO DELLE
PIETRE DURE

★
SPEDALE DEGLI
INNOCENTI

4

PALAZZO
MEDICI-
RICCARDI

SAN GIOVANNI

ROTONDA DEL
BRUNELLESCHI

CAPPELLE
MEDICEE

Piazza
Brunelleschi

Piazza Madonna
d. Aldobrandini

★ SAN LORENZO

A

PALAZZO
PUCCI

BIBLIOTECA
LAURENZIANA

B

VIA DEL
CASTELLACCIO

OSPEDALE DI
SANTA MARIA NUOVA

C

MUSEO DI SAN MARCO

GALLERIA DELL'ACCADEMIA

SPEDALE DEGLI INNOCENTI

★ **San Lorenzo** (**C** A4)
→ *Piazza San Lorenzo*
Tel. 055 21 66 34.
Church: Mon-Sat 10am–5pm
Biblioteca Laurenziana:
daily 8.30am–1.30pm.
Chapel of the Princes
(Cappella dei Principi): Tue-
Sun 8.15am– 5pm (1.50pm
public hols)
Behind the unfinished
façade is a wholly Renaissance church (1419–69).
Brunelleschi designed the
sacristy, where the pure
geometric forms exude a
sense of space, rhythm and
severity. The nave contains
works by Donatello, Lippi,
Bronzino and Rosso. To the
right, on the way out, there
is a cloister and Michel-

angelo's stately staircase
leading up to the Medici
library (Biblioteca
Laurenziana), an opulent
setting for a fine collection.
Michelangelo also
designed the Medici
funerary chapel (Cappella
dei Principi), where the
stunnings tombs and floor
in *pietra dura* (stones of all
colors cut small and inlaid
like mosaics) make you
wonder where exactly does
architecture stop and
sculpture begin.
★ **Palazzo Medici-
Riccardi** (**C** A4)
→ *Via Cavour, 3*
Tel. 055 276 03 40
Thu-Tue 9am–7pm
The stately palace of

Cosimo the Elder was
commissioned in 1444 from
Michelozzo, his favorite
architect. This Renaissance
gem became a widely
copied model throughout
Italy from the 15th century
onward. It has an inner
courtyard and garden, a
baroque reception room
painted by Giordano and,
above all, a chapel with
Benozzo Gozzoli's
wonderful frescos, at first
glance a *Calvacade of the
Magi*, but teeming with
details about court life.
★ **Cenacolo di Santa
Apollonia** (**C** B3)
→ *Via XXVII Aprile, 1*
Tel. 055 238 86 07
Daily 8.15am–1.50pm

Closed 2nd and 4th Mon
A sense of dramatic power
and Benedictine austerity
find striking expression in
the *Last Supper* (1456)
by Andrea del Castagno,
a popular subject for
monastery refectories
(*cenacoli*).
★ **Chiostro dello Scalzo**
(**C** C3)
→ *Via Cavour, 69*
Tel. 055 238 86 04
Mon, Thu, Sat 8.15am–2pm
This Intimist cloister has a
grisaille (gray monochrome
series of frescos painted by
Andrea del Sarto (16th
century) and his pupil
Franciabigio. Taking his cue
from Michelangelo, he
imbued these scenes from

OGNISSANTI ★

Piazza d'Ognissanti

SAN PAOLINO

SAN GAETANO

MUSEO
M. MARINI ★

PALAZZO
STROZZI ★

PALAZZO
VECCHIETTI

PESCAIA DI
SANTA ROSA

OSPEDALE
DI SAN GIOVANNI
DI DIO

V. DE' FOSSI

PAL.
RUCELLAI ★

V.D. PALCHETTI

VIA DELLA VIGNA NUOVA

LOGGIA
D. RUCELLAI ★

VIA
TORNABUONI

Piazza
Strozzi

POSTE
E TELEGRAFI

Piazza
C. Goldoni

PALAZZO
RICASOLI

PALAZZO
CORSINI ★

PONTE ALLA
CARRAIA

LUNGARNO V. PARIONCINO V.D. PARIONE

SANTA
TRINITA ★

PALAZZO
BARTOLINI-
SALIMBENI ★

VIA
PORTA ROSSA

4

FREDIANO
CESTELLO

SODERINI

Corsini

V. D. TERME

PALAZZO
DAVANZATI ★

Piazza
N. Sauro

CHIESA
PRESBITERIANA

MUSEO
FERRAGAMO ★

BORGO SANTI APOSTOLI

SANTI
APOSTOLI

N FREDIANO   D

PONTE SANTA
TRINITA

E   F

MUSEO FERRAGAMO   SANTA TRINITÀ   PALAZZO DAVANZATI

from the Piazza Antinori to the Santa Trinità bridge. The austere Renaissance palace belonging to the wealthy Antinori family of vineyard owners forms a striking contrast to the lavish baroque church of San Gaetano. Nᵒˢ 19, 16, 15, 12, 7, 5 and 3 are also worth a look. In the middle, an attractive early 20th-century loggia precedes the façade of the Strozzi Palace. To the left of the Roman column topped by the figure of justice, stands the Palazzo Bartolini-Salimbeni (16th century).

★ **Palazzo Strozzi** (**B** F4)
→ *Piazza Strozzi*
Tel. 055 239 85 63

Mon-Sat 8am–7pm
A perfect example of Florentine Renaissance, this palace was built for the wealthy Filippo Strozzi by Benedetto da Maiano and Simone del Pollaiuolo ('Il Cronaca'). The palace has a monumental façade, rusticated masonry and a massive projecting cornice. The inner courtyard is completely enclosed, like a small city within a city. The palace is nowadays used for art exhibitions and fashions shows.

★ **Santa Trinità** (**B** F4)
→ *Piazza di Santa Trinità*
Tel. 055 21 69 12
Mon-Sat 8am–noon, 4–6pm;
Sun 4–6pm

The Mannerist façade of this church conceals a simple monastic interior dating from the 11th–14th centuries, which is highly conducive to meditation. Out of the shadows looms the *Annunciation* by Lorenzo Monaco (fourth chapel on the right) and works by Ghirlandaio (chapel to the right of the altar) which depict the Piazza di Santa Trinità and the city of Florence.

★ **Museo Ferragamo** (**B** F4)
→ *Via Tornabuoni, 2*
Tel. 055 336 04 56
Mon-Fri 9am–1pm, 2–6pm
In the impressive medieval Palazzo Spini-Ferroni,

above the stores of the famous shoemaker Ferragamo, is a museum that exhibits some of the extraordinary models worn by various American stars.

★ **Palazzo Davanzati** (**B** F4)
→ *Via Porta Rossa, 9-13*
Tel. 055 238 86 10
Closed for restoration until further notice
On the edge of the medieval district, this stark medieval residence displays a transitional style, part-way between the tower house of the Middle Ages and the seigniorial palace of the Renaissance. Entering the palace is like stepping back in time.

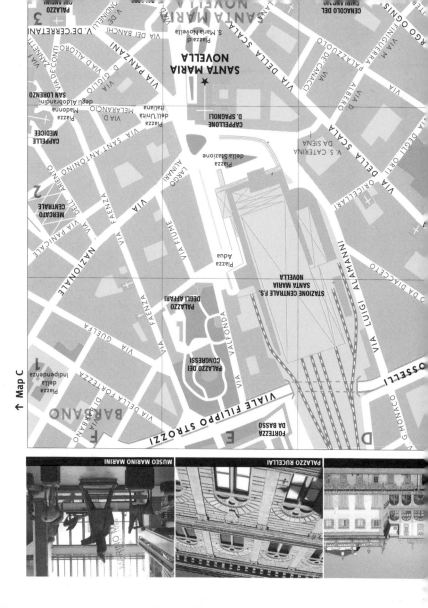

CAPOCACCIA

BP STUDIO

ALICE ATELIER

CAFÉS

Rondinelli (B F3)
→ Via de'Rondinelli, 5r
Tel. 055 28 71 22.
Mon-Sat 7am–7pm
A local café, ideal for
a quick coffee or hot
chocolate in company
with Florentines who are
enjoying a snack of pasta
or salad at the counter or
sitting down.

Caffè Curtatone (B C3)
→ Borgo Ognissanti, 167r
Tel. 055 21 07 72
Wed-Mon 7am–1am
At breakfast time, the
Florentines cluster at
the counter to enjoy a
homemade pastry and
coffee. At lunch time, they
have a bowl of pasta and,
in the evening, a negroni
(Campari, gin and
Martini). Vaulted ceiling
and traditional frescos.

BARS, THEATERS, CLUBS

Procacci (B F3)
→ Via Tornabuoni, 64r
Tel. 055 21 16 56. Daily
10.30am–8pm. Closed Sun
This delicatessen is an
institution when it comes
to truffles. They are sold
fresh (Sep–Dec), in sauce
or as a sandwich filling
(1.30 €). Wonderful with
a glass of wine.

Capocaccia (B E4)
→ Lungarno Corsini, 12-14r
Tel. 055 21 07 51
Daily noon–2am
This bar, with its stylish
décor, is a popular place
to enjoy an aperitif:
unlimited substantial
crostini served with all
types of sauce and an
Italian bitter-based
cocktail (like Campari). In
winter, chart music at top
volume. In summer,
people sit beside the
Arno river. Delicious
cocktails 5–6 €.

Teatro Comunale (B B3)
→ Corso Italia, 16
Tel. 055 21 11 58/35 35. Tue-
Fri 10am–4.30pm (1pm Sat)
In May, this theater is the
seat of the Maggio
Musicale Fiorentino, one
of the oldest music
festivals in Europe, along
with Bayreuth and
Salzburg. It also stages
operas and ballets in the
fall and a symphonic
season in winter. This
venue has often made its
mark on the history of
music and stagecraft.
Fellini himself once made
a guest appearance here.

Meccano (B A2)
→ Viale degli Olmi, 1
(at the entrance to the
Parco delle Cascine)
Tel. 055 331 371
Tue, Thu-Sat 11pm–4am
Dance in the most
famous club in the city, a
popular night out for the
younger crowd. Mainly
the latest chart music.
In summer, there is an
open-air dance floor.
Admission 10 €.

SHOPPING

BP Studio (B F4)
→ Via della Vigna Nuova,
15r. Tel. 055 21 32 43
Mon 3–7.30pm;
Tue-Sat 10am–7.30pm
Ultra-creative fashions for
men and women in this
street lined with stores.
It's probably best not to
look too closely at the
price tags.

Exante (B F4)
→ Via della Vigna Nuova,
16r. Tel. 055 28 29 61
Mon 3–7.30pm;
Tue-Sat 9.30am–7.30pm
A wide selection of
leather bags by famous
and not so famous
designers. Bag 75–150 €.
If you like bright colors,
try Leoncini at n° 44r.

Le Stanze (B D3)
→ Borgo Ognissanti, 50-
52r. Tel. 055 28 89 21
Tue-Sat 10am–1pm, 3.30–
7.30pm; Mon 3.30–7.30pm
Dream décor: you'll want
to buy everything, from
furniture to crockery.
Italian design from the

1960s to the present day.

Officina de Santa Maria Novella (B E3)
→ Via della Scala, 16r
Tel. 055 21 62 76
Daily 9.30am–7.30pm
Closed Sun, Nov, Jan–Feb
Founded in 1612, this is
one of the oldest and most
opulent pharmacies in
Europe. Something of a
museum; come just for a
look, or treat yourself to
something from the range
of essential oils, perfumes,
soaps or even sweets: the
Queen of England shops
here, so it must be special.

Alinari (B F2)
→ Largo Alinari, 15
Tel. 055 23 951
Mon-Fri 9am–1pm, 2–6pm;
Sat 9am–1pm, 3.30–7.30pm
Choose a fascinating
reproduction of forgotten
Florence from the ancient
photo collection dating
back to 1852. Contact
printing and a unique
collotype process.

Alice Atelier (B F2)
→ Via Faenza, 72r
Tel. 055 28 73 70
Daily 9am–1pm, 3.30–
7.30pm. Closed Sun
The carnival is no more,
but in this store the
technique of papier mâché
has been handed down
from father to daughter.
Artistic designs inspired
by the commedia dell'arte.

Santa Maria Novella is an essential part in the study and discovery of Renaissance Florence. Also, like Santa Trinità or Ognissanti, the imposing church contains some fine 15th-century scenes of Florentine life by Ghirlandaio. The district, stretching between the station in the north and the embassies and grand hotels in the southwest, is popular with visitors. To the west, Florentines flock to the Parco delle Cascine on Tuesdays for the market. In the east, around the Via Tornabuoni, the stately palaces are home to fashion houses. In the southeast, the Borgo Santi Apostoli and the Via delle Terme seem caught in a time warp, with their 13th-century fortified tower houses.

I' VINAINO   IL LATINI

RESTAURANTS

Tripes (B D3)
→ *Via M. Finiguerra, next to the Fulgor movie theater*
Daily 8–4am
One of those makeshift booths that perpetuate the working-class tradition of Florentine tripe. Craftsmen and businessmen share tables to devour intestines and other types of offal, any time of day or night. Portion 4 €.

I' Vinaino (B D3)
→ *Via Palazzuolo, 124r*
Tel. 055 29 22 87
Daily 10.30am–midnight
Closed Sun
Good café with a regular clientele of local office-workers and shop assistants. Homemade dishes at unbeatable prices. Menu 8 €.

Trattoria Guelfa (B F1)
→ *Via Guelfa, 103r*
Tel. 055 21 33 06
Daily noon–2.30pm, 7–10.30pm. Closed Wed and Aug
Claudio, Alberto and Rosa are three good reasons to visit this restaurant near the station. Laid-back décor: paintings, old farm tools, tablecloths and paper napkins. Chicken in mushroom sauce is a specialty. Menu 8 €.

Il Latini (B E4)
→ *Via dei Palchetti, 6r*
Tel. 055 210 916
Tue-Sun lunch and evening
Rustic *trattoria* in the annexes of the Rucellai Palace. Always packed, and for good reasons: cooking is the vocation of the whole family, which serves up some excellent Tuscan dishes. Reservation essential (7.30pm or 9.30pm). À la carte 15 €–20 €.

Coco Lezzone (B E4)
→ *Via del Parioncino, 26r*
Tel. 055 28 71 78
Daily noon–2.30pm, 7–10.30pm. Closed Tue evening and Sun
This restaurant serves heavenly Tuscan cuisine. Chunky vegetable soup, meats served in rich sauces, artichokes in lemon. À la carte 20 €.

La Nandina (B F4)
→ *Borgo Santi Apostoli, 64r*
Tel. 055 21 30 24 / Daily 12.30–3pm, 7.30–10.30pm. Closed Mon lunch and Sun
Near the Via Tornabuoni, this restaurant provides an excellent cuisine in a traditional atmosphere. The *antipasti* and desserts are brought to your table on a trolley. *Pappa al pomodoro, ravioli tartufati.* Attentive service. À la carte 20 €.

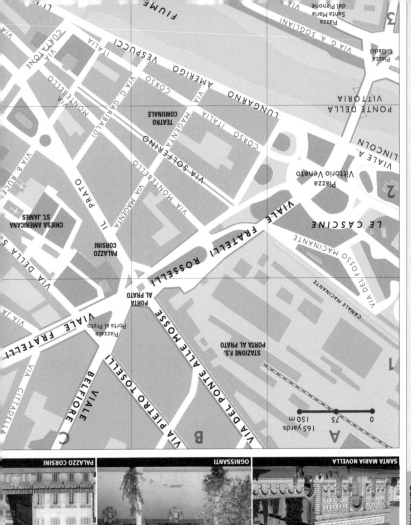

SANTA MARIA NOVELLA

OGNISSANTI

PALAZZO CORSINI

FIUME

Piazza
Santa Maria
del Pignone

VIA G. A. SOGLIANI

Piazza
T. Gaddi

PONTE DELLA
VITTORIA

VIALE A.
LINCOLN

LUNGARNO AMERIGO VESPUCCI

CORSO ITALIA

VIA G. GARIBALDI

VIA MAGENTA

CORSO ITALIA

VIA MONTEBELLO

VIA MAGENTA

VIA SOLFERINO

TEATRO
COMUNALE

VIA MONTEBELLO

Piazza
Vittorio Veneto

LE CASCINE

VIALE FRATELLI ROSSELLI

VIALE DEL FOSSO MACINANTE

CANALE MACINANTE

VIA DEL FOSSO MACINANTE

VIA RUCEL

VIA DELLA S

VIA JA

CHIESA AMERICANA
ST. JAMES

IL PRATO

VIA PRATO

PALAZZO
CORSINI

PORTA
AL PRATO

PORTA AL PRATO

VIALE FRATELLI

Piazzale
Porta al Prato

STAZIONE F.S.,
PORTA AL PRATO

VIA CITTADELLA

VIALE
BELFIORE

VIA PIETRO TOSELLI

VIALE DEL PONTE ALLE MOSSE

165 yards 150 m

75

0

A

B

C

1

2

3

VIA TORNABUONI

PALAZZO STROZZI

★ Santa Maria Novella (B E3)

→ Piazza di S. Maria Novella
Tel. 055 21 59 18
Daily 9.30am–4.30pm; Fri & Sun 1–4.30pm. Cloister: daily 9am–2pm. Closed Fri
Santa Maria, near the station, has a spectacular Gothic-Renaissance façade (Alberti, c. 1458). The rest is older, in pure Florentine Gothic style, inspired by Cistercian architecture. The church contains some outstanding works: the Trinity by Masaccio (dated 1427), the first experimental use of perspective in painting, a crucifix carved by Brunelleschi and one painted by Giotto. Frescos by Lippi and Ghirlandaio, respectively in the Filippo Strozzi and Tornabuoni chapels.

★ Ognissanti (B D3)

→ Borgo Ognissanti, 42
Tel. 055 239 87 00
Church: daily 8am–noon, 4–7pm. Cenacolo: Mon, Tue, Sat 9am–noon
This square lies at the heart of a district of antique dealers. In the 11th century, this was where the Benedictines developed the woolen cloth industry, bringing about the city's expansion. The baroque façade of the church conceals a fine fresco by Botticelli. Ghirlandaio's Last Supper is in the refectory (through the cloister).

★ Palazzo Corsini (B E4)

→ Lungarno Corsini, 10
By appt on 055 21 89 94
Entrance Via del Parione, 11
The finest residence on the embankment, this palace is a perfect example of Florentine baroque. Its terraces, adorned with statues, overhang the Arno river. At the top of the sweeping staircase there is a unique collection of Florentine, Neapolitan and Bolognese paintings.

★ Palazzo Rucellai (B E4)

→ Via della Vigna Nuova, 18
This elegant Renaissance palace is closed to the public. The façade (1446), however, is worth a look with its regular interplay of vertical pilasters inspired by Vitruvius' Rome: a fine example of Alberti's talent.

★ Museo Marino Marini (B E3)

→ Via della Spada
Tel. 055 21 94 32
Daily 10am–5pm (1pm Sun)
Closed Tue and Aug
Modern in content and presentation. One of the few museums in Florence devoted to a 20th-century artist: Marino Marini, key figure of Italian sculpture.

★ Via Tornabuoni (B F4)

The city's smartest shopping street. All the big names in Italian fashion can be found on this avenue, which stretches

MUSEO DI STORIA DELLA SCIENZA

GALLERIA DEGLI UFFIZI

museum above the church.

★ Piazza della Signoria (A B4)

The political and civic hub of Florence since the 13th century is dominated by the Palazzo Vecchio. Beside it and in the Loggia dei Lanzi, you can see what amounts to an amazing open-air museum of Renaissance sculpture (with Cellini's *Perseus*).

★ Palazzo Vecchio (A C4) (Palazzo della Signoria)

→ *Piazza della Signoria*
Tel. 055 276 82 24
Mon-Wed, Fri-Sat 9am-7pm
(11pm Mon & Fri in summer);
Thu and Sun 9am-2pm
The military air of the palace, built to house the government in the 13th century, gives no hint of Vasari's lavish 16th-century remodeling of the interior for Cosimo I, glorifying the Medici who founded the Republic of Tuscany. The walls and ceilings of the Hall of the Five Hundred are covered with frescos by Vasari illustrating the theme of victory over Pisa and Siena.

★ Bargello (A D4)

→ *Via del Proconsolo, 4*
Tel. 055 238 86 06
Daily 8.15am-1.50pm. Closed 1st, 3rd and 5th Sun, 2nd and 4th Mon of the month
The leading museum of major Renaissance works of sculpture and ceramics: Donatello, Michelangelo, Verrochio, Brunelleschi.

★ Museo di Storia della Scienza (A C6)

→ *Piazza de Giudici, 1*
Tel. 055 239 88 76
Tue, Thu, Sat 9.30am-1pm;
Mon, Wed, Fri 2-5pm
Besides other pieces of scientific equipment, the austere Palazzo Castellani has the telescope with which Galileo discovered Jupiter's satellites.

★ Galleria degli Uffizi (A B5)

→ *Piazzale degli Uffizi, 6*
Tel. 055 238 86 51
Bookings on 055 29 48 83
Corridoio Vasariano by appt only 055 265 43 21
Tue-Sun 8.30am-6.50pm
(10pm Sat in summer).
Built by Vasari in 1560 to house the administrative offices (*uffizi*) of the State of Tuscany, this became in 1581 under Francesco I de Medici (1541–87), one of the leading museums in the world. It provides a remarkable overview of Italian painting with works by the country's greatest artists: Botticelli, della Francesca, Lippi, Michelangelo, Pollaiuolo, Uccello, da Vinci, as well as examples of Germanic, Flemish and Dutch work. Vasari's Corridor, linking the Uffizi Gallery to the Palazzo Pitti, offers an unusual view of the Ponte Vecchio and the Arno river.

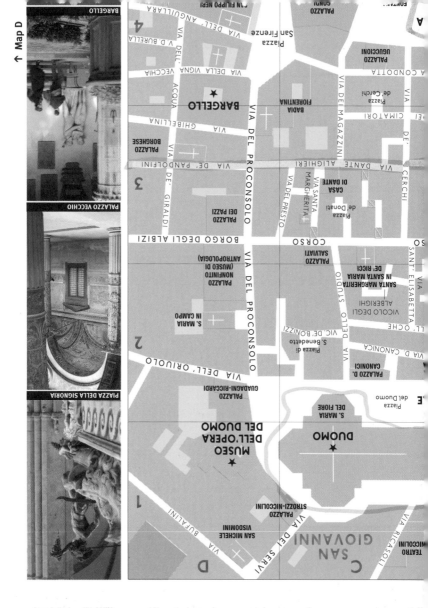

BARGELLO

4

SAN FILIPPO NERI

VIA DELL' ANGUILLARA

San Firenze
Piazza

PALAZZO
FONTANA

A

PALAZZO
UGUCCIONI

A CONDOTTA

VIA DELLA VIGNA VECCHIA

VIA DEL MAGAZZINI

VIA DE' CERCHI

de' Cerchi
Piazza

BADIA
FIORENTINA

★
BARGELLO

ACQUA

VIA GHIBELLINA

PALAZZO
BORGHESE

VIA DEL PROCONSOLO

EI CIMATORI

DE' CERCHI

3

DE' PANDOLFINI

VIA DANTE ALIGHIERI

DE' GIRALDI

PALAZZO
DEI PAZZI

VIA DEL PRESTO

VIA SANTA MARGHERITA

CASA
DI DANTE

de' Donati
Piazza

BORGO DEGLI ALBIZI

CORSO

O S
SANT' ELISABETTA

PALAZZO
SALVIATI

2

PALAZZO
NONFINITO
(MUSEO DI
ANTROPOLOGIA)

VIA DEL PROCONSOLO

VIA DELLO STUDIO

VICOLO DEGLI
ALBERIGHI

SANTA MARGHERITA
IN SANTA MARIA
DE' RICCI

VIA D. CANONICA

VIA S. ELISABETTA

LL' OCHE

S. MARIA
IN CAMPO

VIC. DE' BONIZZI

S. Benedetto
Piazza di

VIA DELL' ORIUOLO

PALAZZO D.
CANONICI

E
Piazza del Duomo

PALAZZO
GUADAGNI-RICCARDI

★
MUSEO
DELL'OPERA
DEL DUOMO

S. MARIA
DEL FIORE

★
DUOMO

1

VIA DEI SERVI

VIA BURALINI

SAN MICHELE
VISDOMINI

PALAZZO
STROZZI-NICCOLINI

VIA DEI CERRETANI

D

C
SAN GIOVANNI

TEATRO
NICCOLINI

VIA RICASOLI

BARGELLO

PALAZZO VECCHIO

PIAZZA DELLA SIGNORIA

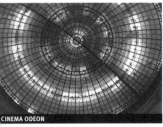

CINEMA ODEON

GIUBBE ROSSE

AL PORTICO

CAFÉS, ICE CREAM PARLORS

Perchè no! (A B3)
→ Via dei Tavolini, 19r
Tel. 055 239 89 69
Daily 10.30am–midnight
Tucked away in an old street in the city center, this modest-looking ice cream parlor has actually been in business since 1939. The homemade ice creams are full of natural ingredients: the pistachio and chocolate flavors are simply wonderful. Perchè no – why not indulge yourself indeed.

Gilli (A B2)
→ Piazza d. Repubblica, 39r
Tel. 055 21 38 96
Wed-Fri 7.30am–10pm;
Sat-Mon 7.30am–midnight
Belle Époque tearoom where the signore come to enjoy the excellent pastries, a house specialty since 1733. Beware, the cappuccino is expensive here.

Rivoire (A B4)
→ Piazza della Signoria
Tel. 055 21 44 12
Tue-Sun 8am–midnight
This confectioner is a Florentine institution, with an unbeatable location, a stone's throw from the Uffizi. But the thing about Rivoire is its deliciously thick hot chocolate.

BARS, MOVIES, CLUBS

I Fratellini (A B3)
→ Via dei Cimatori, 38r
Tel. 055 239 60 96
Daily 8am–8pm
Closed July–Aug
This tiny wine bar, dating from 1875, opens onto the street. Here you can put the world to rights with your neighbors, a glass of the best Chianti in one hand and a panino (roll) filled with porchetta or pecorino cheese in the other. Both 5 €.

Cinema Odeon (A A3)
→ Via degli Anselmi
Tel. 055 21 40 68
This Art Nouveau theater is one of the few movie houses that shows movies in their original language (Mon and Tue).

Giubbe Rosse (A A3)
→ Piazza della Repubblica, 13/14r / Tel. 055 21 22 80
Daily 8am–1am
Intellectuals and artists flock to this friendly literary café to enjoy an aperitif and, later, to hear specialist lectures. Works on the walls are a reminder that this was the birthplace of the Futurist movement (1909). Exhibitions of modern painters as well. Newspapers available.

Astor Caffè (A C1)
→ Piazza del Duomo, 20r
Tel. 055 239 90 90
Mon-Sat 10–3am;
Sun 5pm–3am
At the base of the dome, this café with its metal décor is the meeting place for a trendy crowd that comes here for an aperitif or an after-dinner drink. Concerts in the basement. Crowded at week ends, but friendly atmosphere. Internet access. Cocktails 5 €.

Yab (A A3)
→ Via Sasseti, 5r
Tel. 055 21 51 60
Daily 11pm–4am. Closed Sun and June–Aug
This ultra-fashionable nightclub holds themed evenings and boasts a great atmosphere thanks to good music played by established DJs: house on Tue and '80s hits on Wed. Admission and drink 10–15 €.

SHOPPING

Echo (A D2)
→ Via dell'Oriolo, 37-41r
Tel. 055 238 11 49
Mon-Sat 9am–7.30pm
Designed by an up-and-coming stylist, this line of womenswear is available in two stores, one casual, the other dressy. Very

reasonably priced.

Stefano Veneziani (A C3)
→ Corso, 10r
Tel. 055 21 41 13
Tue-Sat 10am–7pm;
Mon 3.30–7pm
This well-known men's fashion label inhabits one of the beautiful classic stores along the Corso: affordable Italian elegance.

Bizzarri (A C4)
→ Via Condotta, 32r
Mon-Fri 9.30am–1pm, 4–7.30pm; Sat 9.30am–1pm
Herbs, colored flasks and jars: the natural world reduced to powders and elixirs by a herbalist with a magic touch. They can be used for cooking, cosmetics, painting, photography, etc.

Al Portico (A C4)
→ Piazza San Firenze, 1
Tel. 055 21 37 16
Mon-Sat 10am–7pm;
Sun 10am–1pm
A paradise of seeds, earthenware pots, plants and flowers.

Istituto Raffaele (A A4)
Via Porta Rossa, 12
Tel. 055 21 64 60
Mon-Sat 9am–7pm
Closed Sat pm and Mon am
Upmarket beauty treatments from pedicure to manicure in one of the salon's cozy cubicles. 13 –20 €.

Centro Storico

In the high season, Florence's historic center, the area between the Duomo and the Arno river, is packed with tourists, eager to soak up the city's incredibly rich artistic heritage. It was here, in the 14th and 15th centuries, that the Florentine merchants and bankers built ostentatious monuments as proof of their power, financing artists from Giotto to Michelangelo, who were to revolutionize Western art. Attractive pedestrianized streets, lined with luxury stores and stylish cafés, run between the cathedral, the Palazzo Vecchio and the Galleria degli Uffizi. On both sides, quieter medieval lanes reflect the original layout of the Roman city.

CANTINETTA DA VERRAZANO

PERCHÈ NO !

RESTAURANTS

Cantinetta da Verrazano (A B3)
→ *Via dei Tavolini, 18/20r*
Tel. 055 26 85 90
Mon-Sat 8am–9pm
This restaurant, which boasts an attractive traditional décor, serves a range of 100% homemade Tuscan dishes: *focaccia, panino tartufato* and cooked meats. There is seating near the wine cellar (fine Chianti) or you can stand, as people often do in Florence, near the bakery. *Focaccia* 2.30 €.

Giuliano (A C5)
→ *Via dei Neri, 74r*
Tel. 055 238 27 23
Tue-Sun noon–3pm, 5–9pm
Although this restaurant has limited seating, there is a cabinet of mouthwatering Tuscan dishes (soups, vegetables, roast meats), which are very reasonably priced. Choose the wine bar option opposite if you prefer to eat *crostini* at the counter with the regulars. Main dishes 5 €.

The Fusion Bar (A A5)
→ *Vicolo dell'Oro, 3*
Tel. 055 272 66 987
Tue-Fri 3pm–midnight,
Sat-Sun 10am–midnight
The chef at the sushi bar in the ultra-stylish Ferragamo's Gallery Art Hotel is a student of the Shozan school, which subtly marries Japanese and Mediterranean cooking. Both the seating and the décor also show the influence of Japanese esthetics. Terrace on good days. À la carte 15 €.

Da Pennello (A C3)
→ *Via Dante Alighieri, 4r*
Tel. 055 29 48 48
Tue-Sat noon–3pm, 7pm–midnight
The attentive, meticulous service, delicious traditional cuisine and reasonable prices help you forget the crowds of tourists in this medieval district, which still recalls the Florence of Dante and Michelangelo. Menu 16 €.

La Posta (A A3)
→ *Via de' Lamberti, 20r*
Tel. 055 21 27 01
Daily lunchtime and evening. Closed Tue
Enjoy sophisticated Tuscan cuisine in the comfortable dining room of this former coaching inn. Fish specialties (*spaghetti di mare* 7 €). Plush surroundings and a pleasant terrace on a pedestrianized street. Large portions at prices to match. À la carte 30 €.

PIAZZA D SIGNO

PALAZZO DI
Piazza di
Santa Cecilia

CALIMARUZZA

LOGGIA DEL
MERCATO
NUOVO

VICOLO
DEL PANICO

VIA DELLE

PALAZZO
DAVANZATI

VIA PORTA ROSSA

VIA PORTA ROSSA

VIA D

VIA
DEI

V. ARTE
D. LANA

VIA
DE' LAMBERTI

PELLICCERIA

Piazza de'
Davanzati

ORSANMICHELE ★

PALAZZO
DELL'ARTE
D. LANA

CALIMALA

VIA
ORSANMICHELE

VIA S. MINIATO
FRA LE TORRI

POSTE E
TELEGRAFI

VIA DE'
SASSETTI

ANSELMI

SAN CARL
DEI LOMBAR

TAVO

VIA

VICO
DEL BA

Piazza del
Tre Re

VIA DE' MEDICI

VIA D. SPEZIALI

Piazza
della
Repubblica

VIA DEGLI STROZZI

VIA DEGLI

VIA DEI CALZAIUOLI

Piazza
del
Giglio

PALAZZO
VECCHIETTI

VIA DE'

VIA DE' TOSINGHI

VIA DE' TOSINGHI

VIA
ROMA

Piazza d.
Adimari

VIA DEL
CAMPIDOGLIO

VIA DE'
BRUNELLESCHI

VIA DE'
VECCHIETTI

ARCICONFRATE
DELLA MISERIC

LOGGIA
DEL BIGALLO

VIA DE' PECORI

CAMPA ★

BATTISTERO ★

Piazza di
San Giovanni

PALAZZO
ARCIVESCOVILE

Piazza
Olio

SANTA MARIA
MAGGIORE

Piazza
Santa Maria
Maggiore

PALAZZO
ORLANDINI

VIA DE' CERRETANI

VIA DE' MARTELLI

BORGO
SAN LORENZO

VIA F. ZANNETTI

VIA DELL'ALLORO

VIA DE' CONTI

BIBLIOTECA
LAURENZIANA

B

A

BATTISTERO

CAMPANILE

DUOMO

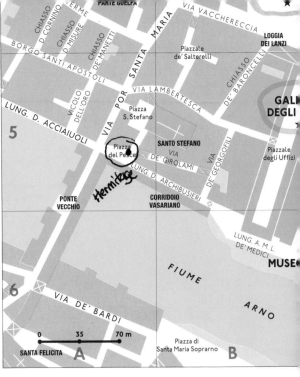

MUSEO DELL'OPERA DEL DUOMO

ORSANMICHELE

★ Santa Maria del Fiore (Il Duomo) (A C1)

→ *Piazza del Duomo*
Tel. 055 230 28 85
Cathedral: Mon-Wed & Fri 10am–5pm; Sun & public hols 1.30–4.45pm; Thu & first Sat of the month 10am–3.30pm
Dome: Mon-Fri 8.30am–7pm (Sat 5pm)

Florentine and Renaissance landmark, and architectural masterpiece, built by Filippo Brunelleschi using neither supports nor scaffolding. When completed in 1436, it surpassed the domes of Pisa and Siena, both in terms of height (328 ft) and diameter (138 ft). At the top of the 463 steps, visitors

can enjoy a 360° panoramic view over Florence. There is a spectacular *Last Judgment* fresco (1579) by Vasari and Zuccari inside the dome.

★ Campanile (A B2)

→ *Piazza del Duomo*
Tel. 055 230 28 85
Daily 8.30am–7.30pm (4.20pm Nov–March)

Graceful, free-standing bell tower, clad entirely in polychrome marble. It took 26 years of work and three architects to complete the campanile, begun by Giotto in 1334. Spectacular view of the nearby dome.

★ Battistero (A B1)

→ *Piazza di San Giovanni*
Tel. 055 230 28 85
Mon-Sat noon–6.30pm;

Sun 8.30am–1.30pm

This 5th-century baptistery, rebuilt in the 11th century, is another Renaissance gem, because of its bronze doors. The sculpted decoration of the south doors are by Andrea Pisano (14th century), while Ghiberti realized the north doors and the exquisite east doors (15th century), known as the Gate of Paradise (Old Testament).

★ Museo dell'Opera del Duomo (A D1)

→ *Piazza del Duomo, 9*
Tel. 055 264 72 87
Mon-Sat 9am–7.30pm; Sun and public hols 9am–2pm

Houses original works from the Duomo, Campanile and

Baptistery that have been removed for protection. It is a must for Michelangelo's *Pietà*, the cantoria (choir loft) by Luca Della Robbia, Donatello's *Mary Magdalene* medallions from the Campanile and the Baptistery doors.

★ Orsanmichele (A B3)

→ *Via dell'Arte della Lana, 1*
Tel. 055 28 47 15 /Daily 9am–noon, 4–6pm. Closed first & last Mon of month. *Museum Mon-Tue 9am, 10am, 11am; Sat-Sun 9am–1pm*

This former grain market was converted into a Gothic church in the 14th century. There are fine statues of the patron saints of the guilds in the wall niches and the

A

PONTE VECCHIO AS SEEN FROM THE UFFIZI

CITY VIEWS

Piazzale Michelangiolo (**F** D2)
Good for an overall idea of the city's layout.
Forte di Belvedere (**F** A2)
A stunning 360° view of the area and grassy lawns for relaxing.
Campanile (**A** B2)
Bird's-eye view of the city, placing the Duomo within easy reach.
Palazzo Vecchio (**A** C4)
An unusual view of the city from the terrace.
Galleria degli Uffizi (**A** B5)
The café affords an unusual panoramic view of the Palazzo Vecchio and the Duomo.

Il caffè

A religion in Italy.
Espresso: strong, black coffee in a small cup
Cappuccino: with frothed milk and chocolate on top
Con latte: milky
Doppio: double espresso
Lungo: weak
Macchiato: with a splash of milk
Ristretto: strong

MUSEUMS

Opening times
→ *Closed Mon or Tue and often in the afternoon*
Visit early in the morning to avoid long queues.
Reservations
→ *Tel. 055 29 48 83*
Advisable in high season for the Uffizi, the Palazzo Pitti, San Marco, the Bargello and the Galleria dell'Accademia.
Concessions
Students: when showing international student card.

Museum passes
→ *The five museums in the Palazzo Pitti and Boboli Garden: 10.35 € (3 days)*
→ *Municipal galleries and museums: 5.15 € entitling the bearer to 50% reduction, valid for a year*
Free admission
EEC members under 18 and over 65.

CHURCHES

Mostly free entry. Coin-operated lighting.
Horaires
→ *Often 9am–noon, 4–7pm*
Dress code
Nothing above the knee.
Gregorian masses
San Miniato al Monte
→ *Winter: daily 4.30pm (vespers) and 5pm (mass); summer: 5.30pm and 6pm*
Duomo
→ *Sun 10.30am*
San Salvatore al Monte
→ *Sun 11am, 5pm (6pm summer)*

GUIDED TOURS

Various organizations offer tours with official guides (brochures available from tourist offices). They are ideal for getting to know the city quickly; also good for visiting museums in greater comfort with pre-booked tickets. Also available: coach trips through-out Tuscany or boat trips on the Arno river.

SHOWS

Listing from the tourist office
→ in the bi-monthly *Florence Concierge Information* (hotels)
→ in the monthly *Firenze Spettacolo* (from newspaper stands) or on
→ *www.firenzespettacolo.it*
Reservations
Box Office (**B** D2)
→ *Via Alamanni, 39*
Tel. 055 21 08 04

SHOPPING

Opening times
→ *Mon-Sat 9am–1pm and 3.30-7.30pm. Closed Mon am (winter), Sat pm (summer), two-three weeks round Aug 15. Food stores closed Wed pm*
Sales
→ *End Jan and July*
Department stores
Coin (**A** B3)
→ *Via del Calzaiuoli, 56r and Via del Corso, 59r*
Tel. 055 28 05 31
Rinascente (**A** B3)
→ *Piazza della Repubblica, 1*
Tel. 055 21 87 65
Supermarkets
Standa (**D** B3)
→ *Via Pietrapiana, 42 / 44*
Tel. 055 234 78 56
Esselunga (**C** E1)
→ *Via Masaccio, 274 / 276*
Tel. 055 573 348

MARKETS

Mercato Nuovo (**A** B4)
→ *Via Por Santa Maria*

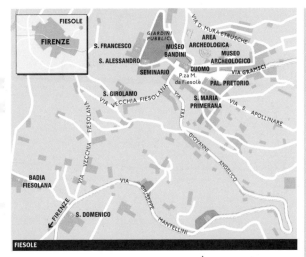

FIESOLE

FURTHER AFIELD

Fiesole
→ *Five miles northeast of Florence, with bus 7 from the station (30 mins); museums closed Tue; market Sat am*

This village on a hill overlooking Florence is a delightful place for a stroll between villas and the fig trees, olive trees and cypresses. The bus stops in a square that affords a fine view of the city whose origins date back to Etruscan times: Teatro Romano, Museo Archeologico, Museo Bandini (Florentine art) and the Duomo. Breath-taking view from Sant' Alessandro; and, on the hilltop the Convento San Francesco. Walking back down along the Via Vecchia Fiesolana, stop at San Domenico (paintings by Fra Angelico) and the Badia Fiesolana (along the road on the right), a Benedictine abbey remodeled by Brunelleschi, with a cloister and a European university (superb view). Catch the bus back from San Domenico.

Certosa del Galluzzo
→ *Four miles south, take bus 36 and 37 from the station. Daily 9am–noon, 3–6pm (5pm winter). Mass first Sun of the month at 11am. Guided tours.*
Imposing monastic site; a fortified Carthusian monastery, built in the 14th century on the orders of St Bruno: choir stalls, Renaissance cloister and frescos by Pontormo.

Mon-Sat 9am–7pm
Or 'Mercato del Porcellino', after the the bronze statue. Leather and souvenirs beneath the loggia.

Mercato delle Piante (A A3)
→ *Via Pellicceria*
Thu 8am–2pm (Sep–June)
Flower and plant market in front of the post office, beneath the porticos.

Mercato delle Cascine (B A2)
→ *Via A. Lincoln*
Tue 7am–1pm
On one bank of the Arno, everything under the sun.

Mercato di San Lorenzo (C A4)
→ *Via dell'Ariento, Piazza San Lorenzo*
Mon-Sat 8.30am–7pm
The best place for leather... try a little haggling. Belts, shoes, bags, clothes.

Mercato Centrale (C A4)
→ *Piazza del Mercato*
Mon-Sat 7am–2pm (and Sat 4–7pm, winter)
Attractive stands selling Tuscan products in a 19th-century covered market.

Mercato delle Cure (C E1)
→ *Piazza delle Cure*
Mon-Sat morning
The most authentic, some way out of the center in the residential district.

Mercato delle Pulci (D C3)
→ *Piazza dei Ciompi*
Mon-Sat 9am–7pm (and last Sun of the month)
Colorful flea market, held between the Loggia del Pesce and the pine trees.

Mercato Sant'Ambrogio (D D3)
→ *Piazza Ghiberti*
Mon-Sat 7am–1.30pm
The most interesting fruit and vegetable market within Florence's walls.

Mercato Santo Spirito (E D2)
→ *Piazza Santo Spirito*
Mon-Sat morning
Sells everything and, on the second Sun of the month, a flea market

(alternating with Ciompi or the Fortezza da Basso).

GREEN SPACES

Parco delle Cascine (B A2)
Two miles of rare trees, cafés, restaurants, tennis, swimming pool, a market, a hippodrome. At one end, there is a remarkable 19th-century Indian mausoleum.

Giardino dei Semplici (C C3)
→ *Via P. A. Micheli, 3*
Mon-Fri 9am–1pm
Founded in 1545 by Cosimo I de Medici for medicinal purposes, this is the third oldest botanical garden in the world, with a cold house and a tropical house. The small park maintains its original layout and contains medical herbs.

Boboli Garden (E E3)
→ *Daily 8.15am–7.30pm (4.30pm winter)*
An oasis of greenery, with statues, on a hillside.

IL VEGETARIANO

CAFFELATTE

ALL'ANCORA SECCA

Treat yourself to a succulent cut of meat in typically Florentine company. Everything on the menu in this restaurant is exquisite. Dishes 11–13 €.

CAFÉS, PATISSERIES

Caffelatte (C C4)
→ *Via degli Alfani, 39r*
Tel. 055 24 78 878
Daily 8am–midnight
Closed Sun
The owner, a past master at making coffee, has given this former dairy a new lease of life. Delicious cakes and very good coffee indeed.

Robiglio (C C4)
→ *Via dei Servi, 112r*
Tel. 055 212 784
Mon-Sun 7.30am–7.30pm
This traditional patisserie has enjoyed an excellent reputation since 1928. Specialty: la *torta campagnola*, pine seed and almond shortbread and cake made with chestnut flour: delicious.

BARS, WINE BARS, CLUBS

Fratelli Zanobini (C A4)
→ *Via Sant'Antonino, 47r*
Tel. 055 239 68 50
Daily 8am–2pm, 3.30–8pm.

Closed Sun
A wine cellar stocking the best Chianti (from Vernaccia to Brunello). Glass of wine 1 –5 €.

Caracol (C C4)
→ *Via de' Ginori, 10r*
Tel. 055 21 14 27
Tue-Sun 5.30pm–1.30am (2.30am Fri-Sat)
This *caliente* Mexican bar is buzzing when it's time for an aperitif: *aficionados* congregate at the counter to sip a marguarita or tequila. Both the music and décor have a distinctly Latin feel. Flamenco on Sun, concerts on Wed.

Rubirosa (C A2)
→ *Viale F. Strozzi, 18-20r*
Tel. 055 230 28 85
Tue-Sun 8–2am
In front of the monumental Fortezza da Basso (16th century), this sophisticated bar is an up-market meeting place for night owls preparing to hit the town. Beer 4 €.

Club Badu (C B2)
→ *Via Zanobi, 114b*
Tel. 055 830 35 13
Wed-Sun 10.30pm–4am
Formerly Soulciety, the Florentine soul club, this venue has changed tempo and now plays hip-hop, reggae and funk. It was good fun before, we hope it will still be now.

SHOPPING

All'Ancora Secca (C A4)
→ *Via de' Ginori, 21r*
Tel. 055 21 64 23
Mon 3–7pm; Tue-Sun 10am–2pm, 3–7pm
Beautifully designed diaries, albums and notebooks bound by Antonella's nimble fingers. Intricately designed clasps, soft leather, warm colors and marbled paper.

La Ménagère (C A4)
→ *Via de' Ginori, 8r*
Tel. 055 21 38 75
Mon 3.30–7.30pm; Tue-Sat 9am–1pm, 3.30–7.30pm
This well-established store, founded in 1896, sells ultra-modern household goods: from traditional utensils to the latest in designer appliances; stocks all you need for successful Italian cookery.

Antica Occhialeria (C C1)
→ *Via San Gallo, 130r*
Tel. 055 47 30 55
Tue-Sat 9.30am–7.30pm
The place for sunglasses, an accessory no self-respecting Italian is seen without. This optician revamps the chic styles of the 1950s–70s with vivid frames. Pair 49 €.

Renato (C C1)
→ *Via San Gallo, 199r*
Tel. 055 48 35 48
Mon-Sat 9am–6pm
A stylish cut in unique surroundings: two white metal floors, futurist hairdryers and art shows. The staff lavishing attention on customers reputedly work for the best hairdresser in Florence. The price of beauty: 80 €.

Da Fernando (C D1)
→ *Via Don Minzoni, 38r*
Tel. 055 58 75 40
Mon-Sat 7am–7.30pm
Closed Wed afternoon
Go out of your way for this Ali Baba's cave of fruit, vegetables and wine, some distance from the center. The shelves are stacked with appetizing jars of fruit in syrup, vegetables *sotto olio* and truffle-flavored olive oil. Finish off the gastronomic odyssey at the Perseus restaurant, a short distance away (see under 'Restaurants').

Solo Donna (C B3)
→ *Via San Gallo, 43r*
Tel. 055 47 79 18
Tue-Sat 9.30am–1pm, 4–7.30pm. Closed Mon am
Italian shoes for women. Reasonably-priced, given the quality of the leather and the craftsmanship.

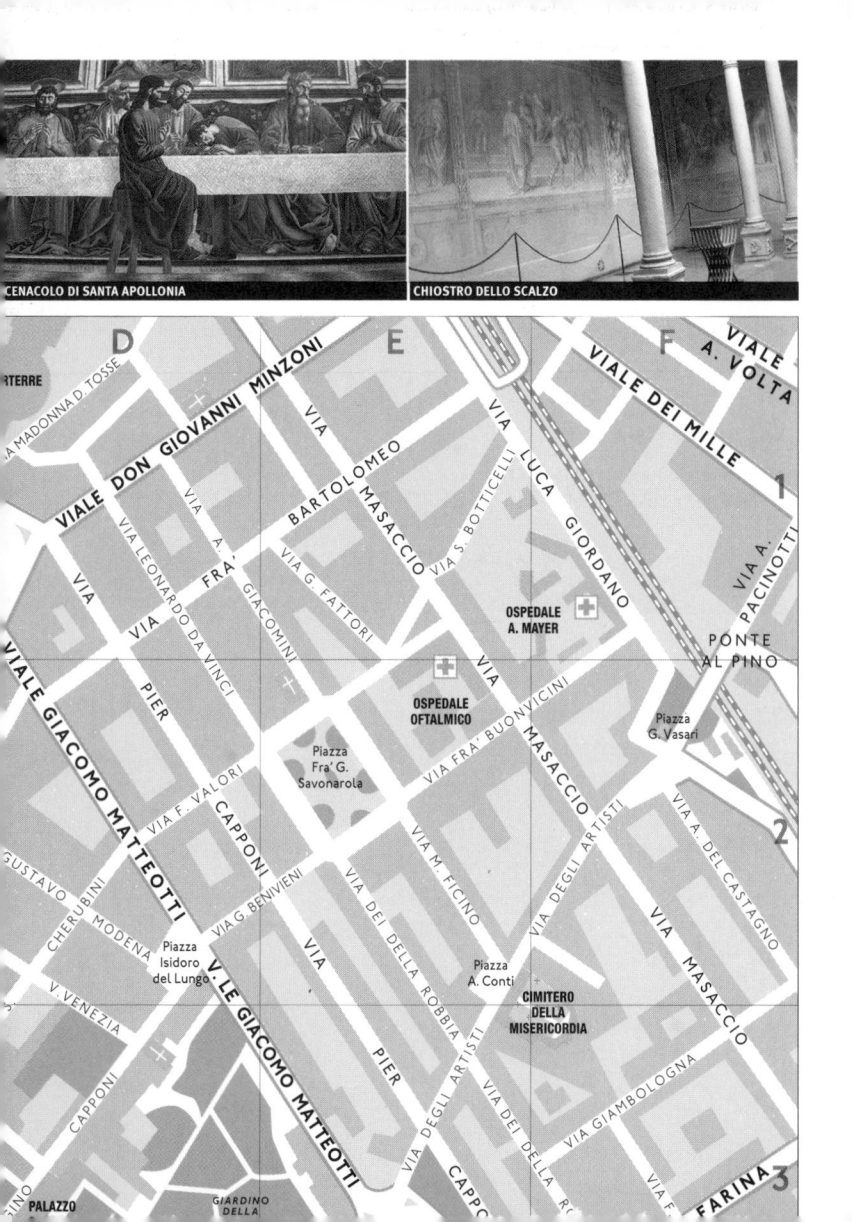

CENACOLO DI SANTA APOLLONIA

CHIOSTRO DELLO SCALZO

CAPPONI

GHERARDESCA

Piazzale
Donatello

VIA GIUSEPPE LA

D. GUERRAZZI

CIMITERO
DEGLI
INGLESI

VIA GIUSEPPE GIUSTI

VIA GIUSEPPE LA

VIALE ANTONIO GRAMSCI

NARDI

VIA JACOPO

V. D. DELLA ROBBIA

VIA BENEDETTO VARCHI

BORGO PINTI

VIA G. GIUSTI

VIA V. ALFIERI

VIA S. PELLICO

VIA LAURA

VIALE B. SEGNI

4

DELLA COLONNA

PINTI

GICO

LA MATTONAIA

Piazza
M. D'Azeglio

BORGO

SANTA MARIA
MADDALENA
DEI PAZZI

D

VIA D. MATTONAIA

E

F

Map D →

PIAZZA DELLA SANTISSIMA ANNUNZIATA

MUSEO ARCHEOLOGICO

he life of St John the
Baptist with an almost
.cultural quality.
★ **Museo di San Marco**
(C B3)
→ Piazza San Marco
el. 055 238 86 08
ue-Sun 8.30am–1.50pm
7pm Sat & Sun)
his serene monastery
ncourages the
ontemplation of the work
f Fra Angelico. The 15th-
century monk and artist
ved here, decorating each
ell with frescos full of grace
nd faith, like his angelic
nnunciation.
★ **Galleria dell'Accademia
Accademia di Belle Arti)**
C BC3)
→ Via Ricasoli, 60

Tel. 055 238 86 09
Tue-Sun 8.15am–6.50pm
(10pm Sat in summer)
In the Academy of Fine Arts
run by Michelangelo, this
collection of sculptures
served as models for
students to copy. Standing
in an immense space are
Michelangelo's audacious
David, realized in his early
period, and his dramatic
Pietà and Four Prisoners,
sculpted when he was
more mature and able to
draw raw emotion from the
rough marble.
★ **Spedale degli
Innocenti** (C C4)
→ Piazza della Santissima
Annunziata, 12
Tel. 055 249 17 08

Thu-Tue 8.30am–2pm
Brunelleschi's hospital
once cared for abandoned
children, as can be seen
from the roundels realized
by the Della Robbias. It is
now a museum with some
moving Madonnas and
Child and a sensational
Ghirlandaio.
★ **Piazza della**   (C C4)
Santissima Annunziata
A typically Renaissance
square by Brunelleschi,
who created a sense of
unity with the slender-
columned porticos. On the
eastern side is the Spedale
degli Innocenti. On the
northern side stands the
church of the Santissima
Annunziata (15th century),

by Michelozzo. This church
was richly decorated in
baroque style, unusual for
Florence, because it
contains a miraculous
painting of the Virgin Mary.
★ **Museo Archeologico**
(C C4)
→ Via della Colonna 38
Tel. 055 23 575. Mon 2–7pm;
Tue, Thu 8.30am–7pm; Wed,
Fri, Sun, Sat 8.30am–2pm
and Sat 8–11pm in summer
Etruscan collection that
dates back to the 9th
century BC: sarcophagi,
cinerary urns and votive
bronzes. Egypt and Greece
are well represented with
priceless vases showing
the influence of Ancient
Greece on Etruscan art.

SAN REMIGIO

MUSEO FIRENZE COM'ERA

D

★ Piazza Santa Croce (D B4)

This spacious square has always been used for public meetings: the Franciscans once preached here beside a small oratory dedicated to the holy cross (*santa croce*), the carnival was held here, as were the matches of *calcio*, a type of very rough soccer, dating back to antiquity and still played in June on the square, in medieval costumes. On the northwest side, a plaque shows the level reached by flood waters in 1966.

★ Santa Croce (D B4)
→ *Piazza Santa Croce, 16*
Tel. 055 24 46 18
Church: Mon-Sat 8am–6.30pm (closed between 12.30 and 3pm in Nov-Feb); Sun 8am–1pm, 3–6pm Cappella dei Pazzi & Museo: Thu-Tue 10am–6pm

This lavishly decorated Franciscan church has become Florence's pantheon: many illustrious figures have been buried here (Machiavelli and Michelangelo). The two chapels to the right of the choir contain frescos, masterpieces by the great Giotto (14th century). In the left transept, the *Crucifix* by Donatello displays surprising realism. To the right of the church, the tranquil cloister leads to the museum (*Crucifix* by

Cimabue) and the Pazzi Chapel (1443–78), a Florentine Renaissance wonder by Brunelleschi.

★ Museo Horne (D A5)
→ *Via de' Benci, 6*
Tel. 055 24 46 61
Mon-Sat 9am–1pm (and 8.30–11.30pm Mon)

A Renaissance palace, bought and tastefully decorated by 19th-century English architect and art historian H. P. Horne. Wonderful furniture and paintings by Giotto, Beccafumi and Lippi. There are some rare capitals in the courtyard.

★ San Remigio (D A4)
→ *Via San Remigio, 4*
Tel. 055 28 47 89

Daily 9–11am, 4–7pm

This church stands in a maze of medieval alleys. An austere and elegant example of Florentine Gothic, its interior radiates a contemplative atmosphere under the Byzantine gaze of a *Madonna and Child* by the school of Cimabue (1360).

★ Museo Firenze com'era (D A2)
→ *Via dell' Oriuolo, 24*
Tel. 055 261 65 45
Fri-Wed 9am–2pm

'The Museum of Florence as it once was'. Fascinating museum charting the urban development of the city from Roman times to the 19th century: maps,

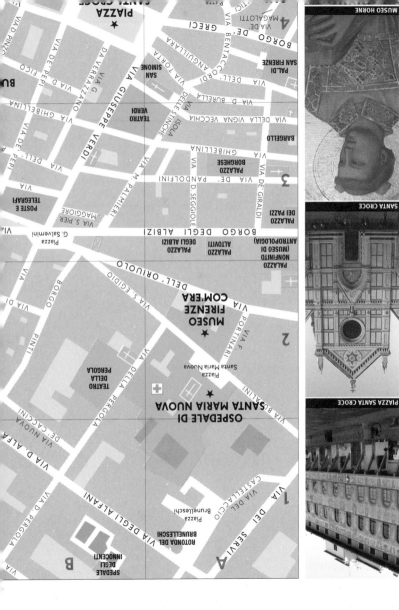

MUSEO HORNE

SANTA CROCE

PIAZZA SANTA CROCE

Santa Croce

This has been the working-class hub of the city for centuries, owing to the large population of leather workers who still ply their trade around Santa Croce and in the medieval streets to the west. The piazza has always been the focus of festivals, games and entertainment of all kinds. In the evening, theaters, jazz clubs, clubs and bars come to life. This district is ideal for window-shopping and people watching, in the Borgo degli Albizi, with its Renaissance palaces, or the flea, fruit and vegetable markets in the east. For art lovers there is Santa Croce, the largest Franciscan basilica in Italy, as well as smaller churches and museums, no less interesting for being off the beaten track.

OSTERIA DE BENCI — MAGO MERLINO TEA HOUSE

RESTAURANTS

Ramraj (D D4)
→ *Via Ghibellina, 61r*
Tel. 055 24 09 99. Daily
10am–3.30pm, 5.30–11pm
A taste of exotic spices in the Tuscan capital: the colors and flavors of India by a chef from Bangalore. Take out or enjoy your meal in the square to the sound of music from the subcontinent (when it isn't drowned out by the TV). Menu 8 €.

Pizzaiuolo (D D3)
→ *Via de' Macci, 113r*
Tel. 055 24 11 71
Mon-Sat 12.30–3pm,
7.30pm–12.30am
The best pizzeria in the city run by Neapolitans who import the mozzarella from their home town. Reservation essential. À la carte 10 €.

Ruth's (D C2)
→ *Via L. C. Farini, 2A*
Tel. 055 248 08 88
Sun-Fri 12.30–2.30pm,
8–10pm
Next door to the synagogue, an orthodox Kosher restaurant for vegetarians bored with the eternal pasta. Fish couscous, Middle-Eastern platter and strudel. À la carte 12 €.

Osteria de Benci (D A5)
→ *Via de' Benci, 13r*

Tel. 055 234 49 23
Daily lunch and dinner.
Closed Sun
This restaurant, opened by a group of friends, has a terrace perfect for warm evenings. Rustic yet sophisticated cuisine: chunky soups, salads and pasta. À la carte 20 €.

La Pentola d'Oro (D C2)
→ *Via di Mezzo, 24r*
Tel. 055 24 18 08
Mon-Sat 7.30–11.30pm
Follow the lead of the garrulous chef, a patriotic Tuscan with impeccable taste, who has dared to reinvent cuisine by referring back to Etruscan history. Your tastebuds will definitely be in for a shock (we're talking wild boar in chocolate!). An institution. À la carte 30 €.

CAFÉS, ICE CREAM PARLORS

Cibreo (D D3)
→ *Via A. D. Verrochio, 5r*
Tel. 055 248 08 88
Tue-Sat 8am–1am
Better known for the legendary restaurant and *trattoria* opposite, Cibreo serves coffee in delicate white porcelain cups. The paneled dining room is cozy in winter. Delicious snacks. Coffee 1.50 €.

ATRO DELLA PERGOLA

JAZZ CLUB

ARTI E MESTIERI

Vivoli (D A3)
→ *Via Isola delle Stinche,*
7r. Tel. 055 29 23 34
Tue-Sat 8am–1am;
Sun 9.30am–1am
The ice cream parlor
to visit in Florence:
deliciously creamy
gelati that make the
long queue worthwhile.

Mago Merlino
Tea House (D C2)
→ *Via de' Pilastri, 31r*
Tel. 055 24 29 70
Daily 5–8pm
Soft music, hookahs,
subdued lighting,
Oriental rugs and quiet
niches: teas from all over
the world, delicious cakes
(5 €)... and, occasionally,
shows in the evening.
Annual (10 €) or weekly
pass (2 €).

BARS, CLUBS, THEATERS

Rex (D B2)
→ *Via Fiesolana, 25r*
Tel. 055 248 03 31
Daily 5pm–3am
Closed June 15–Sep 15
Lighting effects playing
over mosaics : this bar is
a favorite with laid-back
30-somethings when it's
time for an aperitif (2 €),
always served with a
generous helping of
snacks. Great music in
the evening.

Teatro Verdi (D B3)
→ *Via Ghibellina, 91r*
Tel. 055 21 23 20/239 62 42
Mon-Sat 10am–1pm, 4–7pm
Opera house, founded in
1854, puts on eclectic
programs of classical
music, pop and rock.

Teatro della Pergola
(D B2)
→ *Via della Pergola, 12/32*
Tel. 055 22 641
Mon-Sat 9.30am–1pm,
3.30–6.45pm; Sun 10am–
12.15pm. Concerts Sat-Sun
4pm, 9pm
This gem, designed in
1652 for the Great Duke,
is famous as the oldest
theater in Italy. Donizetti,
Verdi and Bellini once
performed here. Fine
programs of classical
music and drama.

Jazz Club (D B2)
→ *Via Nuova de' Caccini, 3*
Tel. 055 247 97 00
Tue-Sun 9.30pm–1am
Closed June–Aug
Since the 1980s, the club
has acquired a proven
track-record with various
international ensembles.
Special guest on Tue.
Membership card 5 €,
beer 5 €.

Maramao (D C3)
→ *Via de Macci, 79r*
Tel. 055 244 341
Tue-Sat 11pm–3am
Closed May–Sep
This club, with its cool hip

Dolce Vita atmosphere,
is packed all night long:
getting onto the dance
floor is something of a
feat on a Sat evening.
Admission 10 €.

Exmud (D A5/B5)
→ *Corso dei Tintori, 4*
Tel. 055 263 85 83
Thu-Sat 11pm–4.30am
Exceptional house music:
electronic, drum 'n bass,
groove, house and video.
Admission 5 –8 €.

Le Murate (D D4)
→ *Via dell' Agnolo*
Tel. 055 239 90 00.
Wed-Sat at 9pm (May 15–
Sep 15)
Former women's prison,
now an open-air venue
for jazz, movies and other
shows (summer). Off the
wall and very popular.

SHOPPING

Arti e Mestieri (D A3)
→ *Borgo degli Albizi, 67r*
Tel. 055 23 47 440
Tue-Sat 10am–7.30pm;
Mon 2.30–7.30pm
Gift ideas for the home
created by imaginative
Italian designers. Soap
dishes masquerading as
fish-filled lakes, snake
shelves, lip ashtrays...

Artigiano Anny (D A3)
→ *Borgo degli Albizi, 45r*
Tel. 055 234 22 26.
Mon-Sat 10.30am–2pm,

3–7.30pm
Gorgeous jewelry made
of crystal and decorated
with ruby red flower
motifs. Rings or earrings
12–30 €.

A piedi nudi nel parco
(D B3)
Borgo degli Albizi, 46r
Tel. 055 234 07 68
Mon-Sat 10am–7.30pm
Closed Mon am in winter,
Sat pm in summer
Alternative fashion
designs by the owner of
the store, and a good
selection of creations by
other contemporary
Italian stylists.

Sbigoli (D B3)
→ *Via San Egidio, 4r*
Tel. 055 24 79 713
Mon-Sat 9am–1pm, 3.30–
7.30pm. Closed Mon am in
winter, Sat pm in summer
Crockery inspired by
Renaissance majolica
and Umbrian or Tuscan
faïence. Dishes, vases
and lamps, mainly made
at the rear of the store.
Affordable prices.

Il Ponte (D C2)
→ *Via di Mezzo, 42b*
Tel. 055 24 06 17
Tue-Sat 4–7.30pm
A politically committed,
modern art gallery. The
son of a printer, Andrea
Alibrandi, publishes
some superb catalogues
himself.

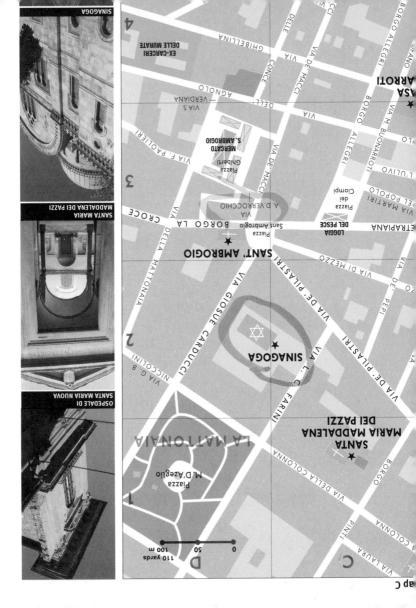

Map of the area showing streets including VIA DI MEZZO, CONCIATORI, VIA DELLE CASINE, VIA PIETRO THOUAR, SAN GIUSEPPE, CE, VIA DEI MALCONTENTI, Piazza Piave, POLI, VIA TRIPOLI, LUNGARNO DELLA ZECCA VECCHIA, TORRE DELLA ZECCA, 5, ARNO, PESCAIA DI SAN NICCOLÒ, 6, CASA SIVIERO, Piazza Giuseppe Poggi, PORTA S. NICCOLÒ, NICCOLÒ, C, D, LUNGARNO B. CELLINI

SANT'AMBROGIO

CASA BUONARROTI

Map F →

models and paintings, including a remarkable sequence of the Medici villas by Justus Van Utens (16th century).

★ **Ospedale di Santa Maria Nuova** (**D** A2)
→ *Piazza Santa Maria Nuova*
The impressive portico designed by Buontalenti in the 16th century adorns the entire façade of the hospital (still operational), founded in the 13th century by Folco Portinari, the father of Dante's beloved Beatrice. The baroque church of Sant'Egidio stands at its center.

★ **S. Maria Maddalena dei Pazzi** (**D** C1)
→ *Borgo Pinti, 58*

Tel. 055 247 84 20
Daily 9am–noon (10.45am Sun), 5–5.20pm and 6.10– 7pm (mass at 5.30pm)
Once through the cloister by Giuliano da Sangallo (late 15th century) and the church with its 17th-century decoration, you enter a hidden labyrinth leading to the Chapter House: this has a *Crucifixion* (1495) by Perugino, which is admirable for its restraint and tenderness.

★ **Sinagoga** (**D** D2)
→ *Via L. C. Farini, 4*
Tel. 055 24 52
Sun-Thu 10am–5pm in April-May and Sep-Oct; until 3pm Nov-March; until 6pm in June-Aug; Fri 10am–1.30pm

This 19th-century building is a marvel of oriental splendor: Byzantine outside, Moorish inside. Florence's synagogue replaced those of the Jewish ghetto that had been situated on the site of the Piazza della Repubblica since the 16th century.

★ **Sant' Ambrogio** (**D** D3)
→ *Piazza Sant' Ambrogio*
Tel. 055 24 01 04. Daily 7.30am–noon, 4.15–7pm
Close by some colorful markets, this 13th-century church (dating back to the 5th) became a eucharistic shrine following a miracle in 1230: it contains an exquisite tabernacle by Mino da Fiesole (1483) to

house the chalice in which the wine was transformed into blood. There are a number of fine frescos and *sinopias* (drafts).

★ **Casa Buonarroti** (**D** C3)
→ *Via Ghibellina, 70*
Tel. 055 24 17 52
Wed-Mon 9.30am–2pm
Michelangelo's memory is preserved in this house, bought before he left for Rome. Superb youthful works, such as the bas-reliefs realized by the 16-year-old genius, who introduced a sense of movement and doubt into the art of the end of the Renaissance: the *Battle of the Centaurs*, the *Madonna della Scala* and a *Crucifix*.

4

VIA UGO FOSCOLO
VIA UGO FOSCOLO
VIA PIETRO METASTASIO
VIA I. PINDEMONTE
VIA V. MONTI
VIA PETRARCA
VIA DE' SERR
VIA ROMANA
VIALE
Piazza
d. Calza
PORTA ROMANA
Piazzale di
Porta Romana

A   B   C

VIA MAGGIO   SANTO SPIRITO

CAPPELLA BRANCACCI

★ **Palazzo Pitti** (E E3)
→ *Piazza de' Pitti*
Tel. 055 238 86 14
Galleria Palatina,
Appartamenti Monumentali:
Tue-Sun 8.30am–6.50pm
(9pm Tue-Fri, 10pm Sat, 8pm
Sun June 15–Sep 15).
Gallerie d'Arte Moderna,
del Costume, Museo degli
Argenti: Tue-Sun 8.15am–2pm
Closed 2nd, 4th Sun and 1st,
3rd, 5th Mon
The grandest of Renaissance
buildings, Palazzo Pitti was
built to plans by Brunelle-
schi that had been rejected
by Cosimo the Elder and
bought by one of his rivals,
the banker Pitti, in 1457.
Later Medici rulers decided
to live there, hence the

luxurious apartments. The
north wing contains the
magnificent collection of the
Palatine Gallery: 25 rooms
packed with Italian paintings
that once belonged to the
grand dukes of Tuscany:
Raphael, Titian and Andrea
del Sarto... An unmissable
complement to the Uffizi's
collections. On the same
floor is the Costume Gallery
and, on the second floor,
the Gallery of Modern Art
(Italian painting from the
late 1700s to the early
1900s). On the ground floor
is the Museo degli Argenti:
a dramatic setting for a
collection of vases, jewelry
and *pietra dura* (hard
stone) mosaics.

★ **Giardino di Boboli** (E E3)
→ *Piazza de' Pitti/Porta*
Romana. Tel. 055 29 48 83
Daily 8.15am–7.30pm
(4.30pm winter)
Formal, Italian-style garden
(16th–17th century). The
natural hills and dales of
the gardens are dotted
randomly with a sculpted
grotto, fountains, statues,
cypress trees and groves.
Stunning views of Florence
and the hills from the
Porcelain Museum, above
the Neptune Fountain and
the Amphitheater.
★ **Museo Zoologico**
della Specola (E D3)
→ *Via Romana 17*
Tel. 055 228 82 51
Thu-Tue 9am–1pm

Designed in the 17th
century for educational
purposes, this collection
of anatomical waxworks is
incredibly realistic and the
largest in the world. This is
not for the squeamish, who
would do better to
concentrate on the
zoological collection.
★ **San Felice** (E D3)
→ *Piazza San Felice*
Tel. 055 22 17 06
Daily 9am–noon, 4–7pm
This unusual, austere 15th-
century façade conceals
some fascinating paintings
a *Crucifix* by the school of
Giotto and a *Madonna* by
Ghirlandaio.
★ **Via Maggio** (E E2)
This road stretches from th

E

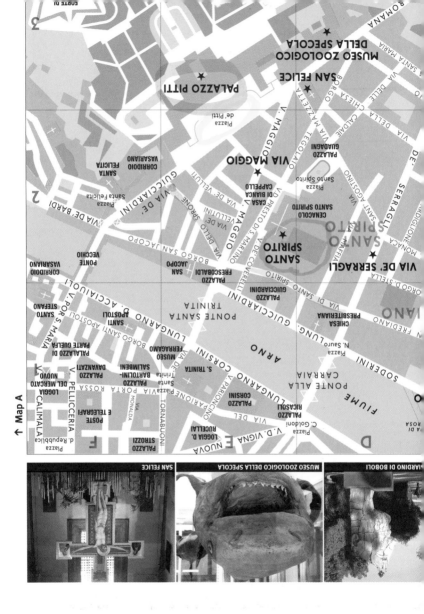

↑ Map A

AFFÈ PITTI

DOLCE VITA

ANTICO SETIFICIO FIORENTINO

Daily noon–2.30pm, 7.30–11pm
Plentiful Tuscan cuisine in a rustic-style dining room: excellent meat and seasonal dishes. The terrace overlooking a quiet square is very popular. Booking essential. À la carte 25 €.

CAFÉS, ICE CREAM PARLORS

Ricchi (**E** D2)
→ *Piazza Santo Spirito, 8/9r. Tel. 055 21 58 64*
Daily 7–1am (9pm winter)
The place to go for cakes, ice creams or a pre-dinner aperitif that can be sipped on the terrace or in the intimate dining room where you can admire the extraordinary plans designed by artists for the façade of Santo Spirito in 1981.

Caffè Pitti (**E** E2)
→ *Piazza de' Pitti, 9*
Tel. 055 239 98 63
Daily 9am–1am
A maze of little rooms and plush sofas. Curl up and savor a *prosecco* (sparkling white wine).

Caffè Artegiani (**E** E2)
→ *Via dello Sprone, 16r*
Tel. 055 29 18 82
Mon-Sat 9am–11pm
For those craving some peace and quiet, this

small two-floor café between the Pitti Palace and the Via Maggio is an ideal stop off; there you can read, write, and enjoy a well-earned rest. Coffee and snacks.

BARS, CLUBS

Dolce Vita (**E** C1)
→ *Piazza del Carmine*
Tel. 055 28 45 95
Daily 5.30pm–1.30am (2am Fri and Sat)
One of the first trendy bars in Florence. It still sets the trend.

Cabiria (**E** D2)
→ *Piazza Santo Spirito, 4r*
Tel. 055 215 732
Daily 8am–1am (2am Fri-Sun). Closed Tue in winter
A must for night owls who enjoy the music's soft beat. Stand between the wall and the bar or relax in the seating area.

Universale (**E** A1)
→ *Via Pisana, 77r*
Tel. 055 22 11 22
Wed-Sun 7pm–3am
Former movie theater, converted into a massive versatile venue: eat, drink, dance or watch concerts and shows.

Sotto Sopra (**E** D2)
→ *Via Serragli, 48r*
Tel. 055 28 23 40
Mon-Sat 6.30pm–2am
One of the best clubs to

visit in the area. Latin beats, house and drum 'n bass in the vaulted cellar. Free admission.

SHOPPING

Francesco da Firenze (**E** D1)
→ *Via Santo Spirito, 62r*
Tel. 055 21 24 28
Mon-Sat 9am–1pm, 3–7.30pm (8pm summer)
Don't be deterred by the badly lit window: the shoes for men and women, handmade by Francesco in the rear of the store, are fabulous. Elegant and perennially fashionable.

Angela Caputi (**E** E2)
→ *Borgo San Jacopo, 82r*
Tel. 055 21 29 72
Tue-Sat 10am–1pm, 3.30-7.30pm; Mon 3.30-7.30pm
Monochrome resin jewelry that sparkles like glass: gorgeous braids and flowers.

Cristina e suoi colori (**E** D1)
→ *Borgo San Frediano, 53r*
Tel. 055 26 86 05
Tue-Sat 10am–1pm, 3.30-7.30pm; Mon 3.30-7.30pm
A lovely jumble of bags, scarves and hats: felt or wool for winter, straw and cotton in summer. Cristina designs and knits the fabrics herself.

Antico Setificio Fiorentino (**E** C1)
→ *Via L. Bartolini, 4*
Tel. 055 21 38 61
Mon-Fri 9am–1pm, 2–5pm
A magical store where the Florentine art of silk-making is still very much alive: Renaissance damasks, brocades and taffetas are woven on 18th-century looms.

Michala Milwertz (**E** C1)
→ *Borgo San Frediano, 159r. Tel. 055 22 96 52*
Tue-Sat 10am–1pm, 3.30-7.30pm; Mon 3.30-7.30pm
A colorful store full of surprises. The vivid colors of Italy combined with the stylish forms of Denmark.

Scaparra Filadelfio (**E** C2)
→ *Via del Leone, 35r*
Tel. 055 28 00 56. Mon-Fri 8am–noon, 2–6.30pm
Wrought iron in all its glory: chandeliers, wall lamps, bed frames, all intricately worked. Adjacent studio.

Valerio Romanelli (**E** C2)
→ *Via del Leone, 43r*
Tel. 055 29 04 86
Mon-Fri 8.30am–12.30pm, 2–7.30pm; Sat 8.30am–12.30pm
Another store-cum-studio devoted to the local tradition of gilded wood: trays, frames, boxes. From luxury goods to reasonably-priced items.

The Oltrarno, or left bank, which was belatedly brought within the ramparts in the 13th century, is more provincial in atmosphere. Although the stately Palazzo Pitti extends the Medici city, the districts of Santo Spirito and San Frediano are still the home of antique dealers and artisans. By day, workshops ring to the sound of tools that once built the beautiful monuments adorning the streets of Florence. The Boboli Garden (Giardino di Boboli) is an impressive example of a Tuscan-style landscaped sculpture gardens. In the evenings, smartly dressed Florentines socialize on the squares and in the restaurants and bars.

OSTERIA SANTO SPIRITO · RICCHI

RESTAURANTS

Da Pruto (**E** C2)
→ *Piazza T. Tasso, 9r*
Tel. 055 22 22 19
Daily lunch and dinner
Closed Mon
Somewhat off the beaten track on a pretty square surrounding a small sport's ground. The atmosphere is cheap and cheerful at lunchtime, and more traditional in the evening. Tasty fish specialties: *tagliatelle all'astice* (lobster). Weekday lunch menu 6–8 €.

Cambi (**E** C1)
→ *Via San Onofrio, 1r*
Tel. 055 21 71 34
Mon–Sat 12.30–2.30pm,
7.30–10.30pm
Tourists and local residents squeeze into this beautiful vaulted dining room plastered with old photos to savor *lardo di collonata* and *trippe alla fiorentina*. Those on a diet shouldn't come here. Terrace in the summer. Booking essential. À la carte 16 €.

Osteria Santo Spirito
(**E** D2)
→ *Piazza Santo Spirito, 16r*
Tel. 055 238 23 83. Daily
12.15–3pm, 7.45–11pm
Multicolored interior, terrace overlooking the delightful Santo Spirito square and a style of cuisine that reinvents traditional Tuscan flavors. This restaurant has a youthful, lively feel – perfect for enjoying a glass or more of excellent wine. À la carte 20 €.

Trattoria Angiolino (**E** D1)
→ *Via Santo Spirito, 36r*
Tel. 055 239 89 76
Daily lunch and dinner
Closed Mon
The floorshow in this restaurant is provided by the kitchens: adorned with old cauldrons and garlands of tomatoes, garlic and corn, this splendid scene can be seen from the dining room. Stylish service and traditional dishes: the delicious rib of beef with *patate all'arrosto* (roast potatoes) is the best in the city. À la carte 20 €.

Trattoria del Carmine
(**E** C1)
→ *Piazza del Carmine, 18r*
Tel. 055 21 86 01. Mon-Sat
noon–3pm, 7pm– midnight
A classy place for an exquisite meal: rabbit with olives, salted cod cooked Livorno style and very good desserts. Excellent Chiantis. Book ahead.
À la carte 20 €.

I Quattro Leoni (**E** E2)
→ *Via de' Vellutini, 1r*
Tel. 055 21 85 62

↓ Map B

PALAZZO PITTI

GIARDINO DI BOBOLI

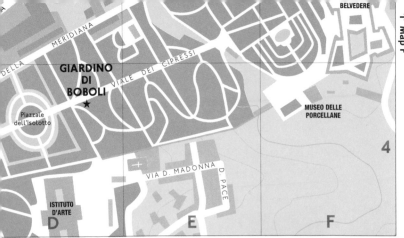

BELVEDERE

GIARDINO
DI
BOBOLI
★

MERIDIANA

DELLA

VIALE DEI CIPRESSI

VIA D. MADONNA

D. PACE

VIA D. MADONNA

Piazzale
dell'Isolotto

MUSEO DELLE
PORCELLANE

ISTITUTO
D'ARTE

D   E   F

4

SAN FREDIANO IN CESTELLO

VIA DE' SERRAGLI

azza San Felice to the anta Trinità bridge, and is dorned with statues of the ur seasons (16th century). n extension of the Via ornabuoni, it has some najestic palaces (n.os 30, 8, 15, 13, 11, 7). The finest alace, at n° 26, decorated ith *sgraffito*, was built by uontalenti in the 16th entury for Bianca Cappello, courtesan and artists' nodel, who became the ife of Francesco de Medici.

★ **Santo Spirito** (**E** E2)
➤ *Piazza Santo Spirito*
el. 055 230 28 85
aily 9am–noon, 4–6pm
enacolo: Tue-Sun 9am–2pm
ree-lined square with narket, cafés and

restaurants. The Palazzo Guadagni and its great loggia (16th century) on the southeast side is worth a look. The 18th-century façade of the church forms a striking contrast with the interior, which is pure Brunelleschi. Sangallo drew his inspiration from the great master for the highly successful sacristy (*Cristo* by Michelangelo). The nave contains a Filippino Lippi, from 1504, while the refectory (to the left of the façade) boasts a *Crucifixion* and a *Last Supper* by Orcagna (1360).

★ **Cappella Brancacci** (**E** C2)
→ *Piazza del Carmine, 14*

Tel. 055 238 21 95
Wed-Mon 10am–5pm; Sun and public hols 1–5pm
To the right of the church of Santa Maria del Carmine, and at the end of the cloister, stands the fabulous Brancacci Chapel. The gracious style of frescos by Masolino and Lippi is in stark contrast to the work of Masaccio, which is remarkable for its mastery of realism and the laws of perspective.

★ **San Frediano** (**E** C1)
→ *Piazza di Cestello, 4*
Tel. 055 21 58 16
Daily 9–11.30am, 4.30-5.30pm (4–5pm summer); Sun 10–11am, 5–6pm
This church is entirely

baroque, except for a *Madonna* with an extremely expressive smile by the school of Pisano (13th century, third chapel on the left).

★ **Via de' Serragli** (**E** D2)
A street full of elegant palaces: n.os 8, 9, 17. At the corner of the Via Santa Monaca, there is a tabernacle by Bicci (1427). At n° 144, there is the Torrigiani Garden. The street runs into the Piazza della Calza, where there is a convent converted into a hotel which boasts a *Last Supper* by Franciabigio (16th century). The Porta Romana was the way out of the city in 1326.

SAN
LEONARDO

SERBATOIO
DI CARRAIA

GALILEO GALILEI

VIALE

VIA GIRAMONTINO

VIA DI SAN LEONARDO

VIA DELL' ERTA CANINA

4

0   75   150 m

165 yards

A   B   C

CASA SIVIERO

PIAZZA MICHELANGIOLO

★ **Ponte Vecchio** (**F** A1)
This bridge, constructed on sturdy pillars, is the only bridge in Florence to have withstood wars and floods since 1345. In the 15th century it was home to a foul-smelling market and was mainly occupied by hog-butchers who would dispose of their waste in the Arno River. In the 16th century, for reasons of hygiene, the Grand Duke removed the butchers and replaced them with goldsmiths. They're still here and today the bridge acts as a magnet for a continual stream of window-shopping tourists. The Corridor (*Corridoio*

Vasariano, see **A** ★) running above the stores was built by Vasari and allowed the Grand Duke to avoid the crowds. There are marvelous views of the Arno and the city from the center of the bridge.
★ **Santa Felicità** (**F** A1)
→ *Piazza Santa Felicità*
Tel. 055 21 30 18
Daily 9am–noon, 3–6pm;
Sun 9am–1pm
The façade of the church on the square is linked to Vasari's Corridor: the Medici rulers could watch services from the inner box. Living in the Pitti Palace since the late 16th century, this became their court church. Inside, the Capponi

Chapel (first on the right) was built by Brunelleschi in 1410, and decorated by the Mannerist painter Pontormo in 1525–28 (his *Deposition from the Cross* is magnificent).
★ **Via de' Bardi** (**F** B1)
This is a narrow, little-known street, where few walkers stroll in the shadow of the tall, austere palaces, brightened by private gardens. N⁰ˢ 36 and 28-30, with their inner courtyards and projecting cornices, are characteristic of the 14th and 15th centuries. On one side, the church of Santa Lucia dei Magnoli (mass 5.30–6pm) contains a *St Lucy* painted

by the Sienese artist Lorenzetti (14th century) and an *Annunciation* by one of Botticelli's studen Don't miss the Mozzi Palace, a typical 13th-century fortress opposite the Bardini Museum.
★ **Museo Bardini** (**F** B2
→ *Piazza de' Mozzi, 1*
Tel. 055 234 24 27
Closed for restoration
This church was converte into a palace in 1881 by a Florentine antique dealer Stefano Bardini. It now displays on four floors an eclectic collection amasse by Bardini: various *objets d'art* from the Middle Age to the baroque era, music instruments, fine

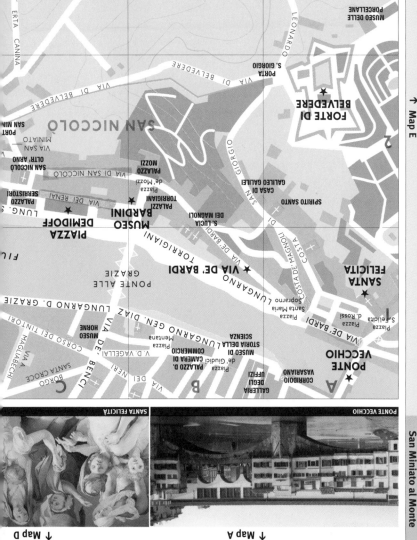

→ Map E

↓ Map A

PONTE VECCHIO

↓ Map D

SANTA FELICITA

F

San Miniato al Monte

Beyond the Ponte Vecchio, in the eastern reaches of Florence, visitors can enjoy a quiet stroll with the city on one side and the countryside on the other. Within the city walls, the streets are home to silversmiths, book-binders, engravers and other craftsmen. They are so peaceful it is hard to believe this is one of the hot spots for Florentine nightlife with some excellent restaurants and bars. Outside the ramparts, the legendary layout of the Renaissance city can be clearly seen: Piazzale Michelangiolo, San Miniato and the Forte di Belvedere are best visited on foot to make the most of the stunning panoramic vistas.

I TAROCHI | VOLPE E L'UVA

RESTAURANTS

Bordino (F A1)
→ *Via Stracciatella, 9r (before the Costa di S. Giorgio). Tel. 055 21 30 48 Mon-Sat noon–2.30pm, 7.30–10.30pm*
You'll get here a good meal at an excellent price: lunch menu 6 €.

I Tarochi (F C2)
→ *Via dei Renai, 12/14 Tel. 055 234 39 12. Tue-Sun 12.30–2.30pm, 7pm–1am*
Pizzas cooked in a wood-fired oven for a tasty snack in a vaulted dining room. Pizza 6 €.

Antica Mescita (F C2)
→ *Via di San Niccolò, 6or Tel. 055 234 28 36 Mon-Sat noon–3.30pm, 7pm–midnight*
Delightful eatery in the crypt of the church of San Niccolò. Dishes 6–8 €.

Enoteca Fuori Porta (F C2)
→ *Via del Monte alle Croci, 1or. Tel. 055 23 42 483 Mon-Sat 12.30–3.15pm, 7.15pm–12.15am*
Halfway up the San Miniato hillside stands this wine store, popular for its cellar and its *crostini* which sport around ten different cheeses with an array of toppings (*caprino, tartufo, prosciutto*). Views over the ramparts. Dishes 8 €.

Volpe e l'Uva (F A1)
→ *Piazza de' Rossi, 1r (after the Piazza Santa Felicità) Tel. 055 239 81 32 Mon-Sat 10am–8pm*
This wine bar is run by a true connoisseur, perfect for lovers of fine wine. It also serves the best Tuscan and French cheeses, as well as delicious cooked meats. Main dish + glass of wine 10–15 €.

Pane & Vino (F C2)
→ *Via San Niccolò, 60/70r Tel. 055 247 69 56 Mon-Sat 8pm–1am*
Elegant, delicious Italian nouvelle cuisine, perfectly complemented by a good wine list. One of the best restaurants in the city. Dishes 13 €.

CAFÉS, ICE CREAM PARLORS

Frilli (F C2)
→ *Via San Miniato, 5r Tel. 055 234 50 14 Thu-Tue 3–8pm (midnight in summer)*
Tiny ice cream parlor that has been handed down from father to son since 1939. The ice creams are deliciously light.

La Loggia (F D3)
→ *Piazzale Michelangiolo, 1 Tel. 055 234 28 32*

SCOOTERS IN FLORENCE

TAXIS

Official taxis are white, with a sign on the roof.
Taxi stands
Stazione, Santa Trinità, Repubblica, Santa Maria Novella, Duomo, San Marco, Santa Croce.
Radiotaxis
→ Tel. 055 42 42/47 98, 43 90/43 86

Fares
→ 5–8 € per journey

CARS

You are only allowed to drive and park in the historic center to get to your hotel. Be warned: there is a highly efficient towing service in operation in the city.
→ Tel. 055 30 82 49
Parking lots
Public parking lots charge less than hotel garages if you are staying for several days.
→ Piazza della Libertà, Piazza Stazione, Fortezza da Basso, Porta Romana...
Car hire
Avis (**B** D3)
→ Borgo Ognissanti, 128r. Tel. 055 239 88 26
Europcar (**B** D3)
→ Borgo Ognissanti, 53
Tel. 055 236 00 72
Hertz (**B** D3)
→ Via Finiguerra, 33r
Tel. 055 28 22 60

e lavishly restored rmer Hotel Splendor, eserves its name, which anslates as: 'The garden the Medici'. All mod ns, marvelous anoramic views and a ower-filled terrace for reakfast in the sun: an asis just a short walk om San Marco. 163–180 €.
avid (**F** F2)
→ Viale Michelangelo, 1 l. 055 681 16 95
ww.davidhotel.com
his comfortable 19th-entury villa with the feel f a family-owned guest-ouse has been handed own through the enerations and is xtremely well run. Well-ept rooms and period rniture. With its own arking lot and garden-errace. 150–186 €.
orre Guelfa (**B** F4)
→ Borgo Santi Apostoli, 8
el. 055 239 63 38
his 13th-century tower

harks back to the cruel days of the Guelphs (supporters of the pope) who defeated the Ghibellines (supporters of the emperor): 15 fairy-tale rooms with a canopy bed. Elegant service. Bar on the top floor with panoramic terrace (March-Oct). 170 €.

EXPENSIVE ...

Monna Lisa (**D** B2)
→ Borgo Pinti, 27
Tel. 055 24 79 751
www.monnalisa.it
The unassuming façade of this Renaissance palazzo hides a hotel of great charm, with wooden ceilings, cotto (terracotta) floors, works of art and antiques (the bar is an old confessional). Ask for a room looking out onto the hotel's greatest asset: a gorgeous garden where breakfast is served in summer. 180–284 €

Torre di Bellosguardo (**E** A3)
→ Via Roti de Michelozzi, 2
Tel. 055 229 81 45
A 15-minute drive from the center, this 16th-century villa, built around a tower, is a haven of cool in hot summer days. Spacious, tasteful, with beautiful reception rooms and bedrooms, ornamental gardens and a swimming pool, staying here is a must. Amazing 360° panoramic views from the top-floor suites. Car essential. 280 €.
Gallery Art Hotel (**B** C2)
→ Vicolo dell'Oro, 5
Tel. 055 27263
www.lungarnohotels.com
Launched by the Salvatore Ferragamo fashion group, this hotel, doubling as an art gallery for contemporary artists, oozes class and slick chic. Moving around leather, wood, wool and stone you become the hero of a design book. 310 €.

OE   ALEXANDRO DARI   IL BISONTE

Behind the Piazzale, this opulent café–restaurant in a neoclassical loggia affords a fantastic view over the city. Ideal for coffee (the meals are a little pricey).

BARS, CLUBS

James Joyce (F F2)
→ Lungarno B. Cellini, 1r
Tel. 055 658 08 56
At the end of the embankment, this real Irish pub with its large tree-lined terrace is very popular on sunny days. Beer 3.50 €.

Il Rifrullo (F C2)
→ Via San Niccolo, 55r
Tel. 055 234 26 21
Daily 8–1am
Open fire in the winter, terrace in the summer and, throughout the year, a long counter made of dark wood covered with snacks for a pre-dinner aperitif. Popular early-evening meeting place for clubbers.

Zoe (F C2)
→ Via dei Renai, 13r
Tel. 055 24 31 11
Daily 9.30–2am
On the Piazza Demidoff, cocktails flow freely in front of a dazzling range of aperitifs. There isn't usually enough space within the red walls to

accommodate the crowds, which spill out onto the terrace.

Montecarla (F B2)
→ Via de' Bardi 62r
Tel. 055 23 40 259
Daily 9pm–4am (5am Fri and Sat)
It is virtually impossible to get into one of the most exuberant bars in the city on a Sat evening: two floors of floral patterns and leopard-print sofas. People come here to curl up and illustrate or color the notebooks on the table. Hefty gin and tonics. Admission and one drink 7.50 €.

Il Jaragua (F C2)
→ Via dell'erta Canina, 12r
Tel. 055 234 36 00
Daily 9.30pm–3am
This is the Latin club in Florence: give yourself over to the heady rhythms of the merengue, chachacha and salsa after a free lesson provided by the club. Free admission.

Caffè la Torre (F E2)
→ Lungarno B. Cellini, 65r
Tel. 055 68 06 43
Daily 11–3am
A popular mecca of Florentine nightlife: for the price of a beer, help yourself to the copious, all-you-can-eat buffet from 7–9pm and take it

out onto the sociable terrace. Evening concerts in the dining room.

SHOPPING

Il Torchio (F B1)
→ Via de' Bardi 17r
Tel. 055 234 28 62
Mon-Fri 9am–7.30pm;
Sat 9.30am–1pm
Once inside, just walk past the shelves to watch the craftsmen painstakingly working with magnificent leather. There is a wide selection of diaries, notebooks, albums and frames. Very reasonable prices.

Lisa Corti (F B2)
→ Via de' Bardi, 58
Tel. 055 264 56 00
Mon-Sat 10am–1pm, 3.30–7.30pm. Closed Mon am
This vibrant store is a riot of Indian colors. Lisa Corti covers a wide variety of household objects in gorgeous fabrics, bringing Indian sophistication into everyday life.

Alexandro Dari (F C2)
→ Via di San Niccolò, 115r
Tel. 055 24 47 47
Mon-Sat 9.30am–1.30pm, 4–7.30pm.
Closed Mon am (winter) & Sat pm (summer)
A jeweler in a class of his own, a world apart from the Ponte Vecchio where

you can find the best and the worst. In this store extraordinary creativity goes hand in hand with passion and culture: inspiration for the rings is drawn from Gothic architecture, castles, alchemy, music, etc.

Il Bisonte (F D2)
→ Via di San Niccolò, 24r
Tel. 055 230 28 85
Mon-Sat 9am–1pm, 3–7pm
A gallery of ancient and modern prints. The name is derived from a work given by Henry Moore to the woman who runs this gallery, Maria Luigia Guaita. There is also a renowned school of engraving at this address.

City Lights Italia (F D2)
→ Via di San Niccolò, 23r
Tel. 055 234 78 82. Mon-Fri 10am–1pm, 2–7.30pm
A bookstore-publishing house where you can read poetry published both in its original language and in Dante's Italian. It holds a poetry festival in July as well as special events in the evening.

Certini (F D2)
→ Via di San Niccolò, 2n
Tel. 055 23 42 694. Mon-Fri 8.30am–12.30pm, 2.30–7pm
Wrought-iron store and studio: objects with finely chased ivy leaves. From subtle to kitsch.

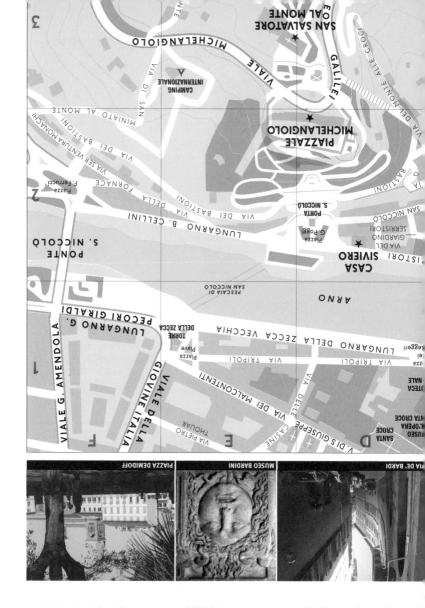

SAN SALVATORE
AL MONTE ★

VIALE MICHELANGIOLO

VIA DEL MONTE ALLE CROCI

GALILEI

VIA INTERNAZIONALE
CAMPING

VIALE

PIAZZALE
MICHELANGIOLO ★

VIA DI SAN
MINIATO AL MONTE

VIA DEI BASTIONI

VIA SER VENTURA MONACHI

Piazza
F.Ferrucci

VIA DELLA FORNACE

VIA DEI BASTIONI

BASTIONI

LUNGARNO B. CELLINI

SAN NICCOLÒ

PONTE
S. NICCOLÒ

PORTA
S. NICCOLO

Piazza
G. Poggi

SERRISTORI
GIARDINO
VIA DEL

CASA
SIVIERO ★ SIRISTORI

ARNO

PESCAIA DI
SAN NICCOLO

LUNGARNO G.
PECORI GIRALDI

TORRE
DELLA ZECCA

LUNGARNO DELLA ZECCA VECCHIA

leggeri
zza

VIA G. AMENDOLA

Piazza
Plave

VIA TRIPOLI

VIA TRIPOLI

VIA DEI MALCONTENTI

GIOVINE DELLA
VIALE
ITALIA

VIA DELLE CASINE

V. DI S.GIUSEPPE

THOUAR
VIA PIETRO

OTECA
NALE

MUSEO
CROCE
L'OPERA
NTA CROCE

SANTA

F   E

1   2   3

PIAZZA DEMIDOFF

MUSEO BARDINI

VIA DE' BARDI

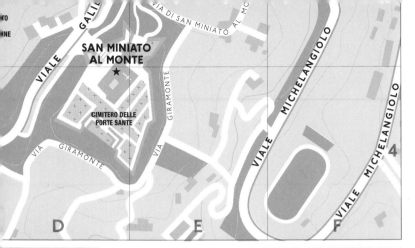

AN SALVATORE AL MONTE

SAN MINIATO AL MONTE

FORTE DI BELVEDERE

rchitectural elements
nd masterpieces painted
nd sculpted by Camaino,
ollaiuolo and Tiepolo.

Piazza Demidoff (F C2)
pleasant square, named
ter a philanthropic
ussian prince, whose
atue stands in the middle
a little garden, where
ou can take time out in
e shade of the trees to
njoy the view over the
rno, the National Library
nd Santa Croce.

Casa Siviero (F D2)
→ Lungarno Serristori, 1-3
el. 055 234 52 19
on 9.30am–12.30pm;
at 3.30–6.30pm
ome of the secret agent
nd art historian who

helped restore the Italian
heritage confiscated by the
Nazis. Statues, paintings
and furniture.

★ **Piazzale
Michelangiolo (F** D2)
→ Take bus 13 or 12
Like the copy of David
oresiding in the square
dedicated to Michelangelo,
it is impossible to tire of
this view: the winding Arno
and, here and there, towers,
domes and campaniles
against the skyline. In the
distance are the mountain-
tops of Fiesole and the
Apennines.

★ **San Salvatore al Monte**
(F E3)
→ Via San Salvatore al
Monte, 9

Tel. 055 234 26 40
Daily 8am–noon, 3–6pm
A peaceful stopping place
before San Miniato. Michelangelo, who was very fond
of the understated two-floor
structure built by Il Cronaca
(1504), nicknamed it 'his
pretty country lass'.

★ **San Miniato (F** D3-4)
→ Via del Monte alle Croci, 34
Tel. 055 234 27 31
Daily summer: 8am–7.30pm
(mass 6pm); winter: 8am–
12.30pm, 2.30–7.30pm
There is a memorable view
from the square in front of
the church: on one side, the
idyllic vista of countryside
and city, and on the other,
the serpentine and marble
façade in pure Tuscan

Romanesque style. From its
delicate marble floor with
symbols of animals and
signs of the zodiac, to
Michelozzo's Cappella del
Crucifisso (15th century),
the interior radiates
spirituality. Look out
particularly for Spinello
Aretino's fine frescos in the
sacristy (14th century).

★ **Forte di Belvedere**
(F A2)
→ Via di San Leonardo
Closed for restoration
A 16th-century bastion:
take a stroll along the Via
del Belvedere and the Via
San Giorgio della Costa
(Galileo's house at n° 27),
with wonderful views:
a true taste of Tuscany.

Transports in Florence

Terminus
Line number
SAN JACOPINO
FORTEZZA DA BASSO
CANALE MACINATE
LE CASCINE
STAZIONE F.S. PORTA AL PRATO
LE CASCINE
STAZ. CENTRALE F.S. SANTA MARIA NOVELLA
S. LORENZO
S. MARIA NOVELLA
FIUME ARNO
S. MARIA NOVELLA
PIGNONE
OGNISSANTI
S. FREDIANO IN CESTELLO
MONTICELLI
SAN FREDIANO
SANTA MARIA DEL CARMINE
SANTO SPIRITO
SANTO SPIRITO
PALAZZO PITTI
GIARDINO TORRIGIANI
GIARDINO DI BOBOLI
GALLUZZO

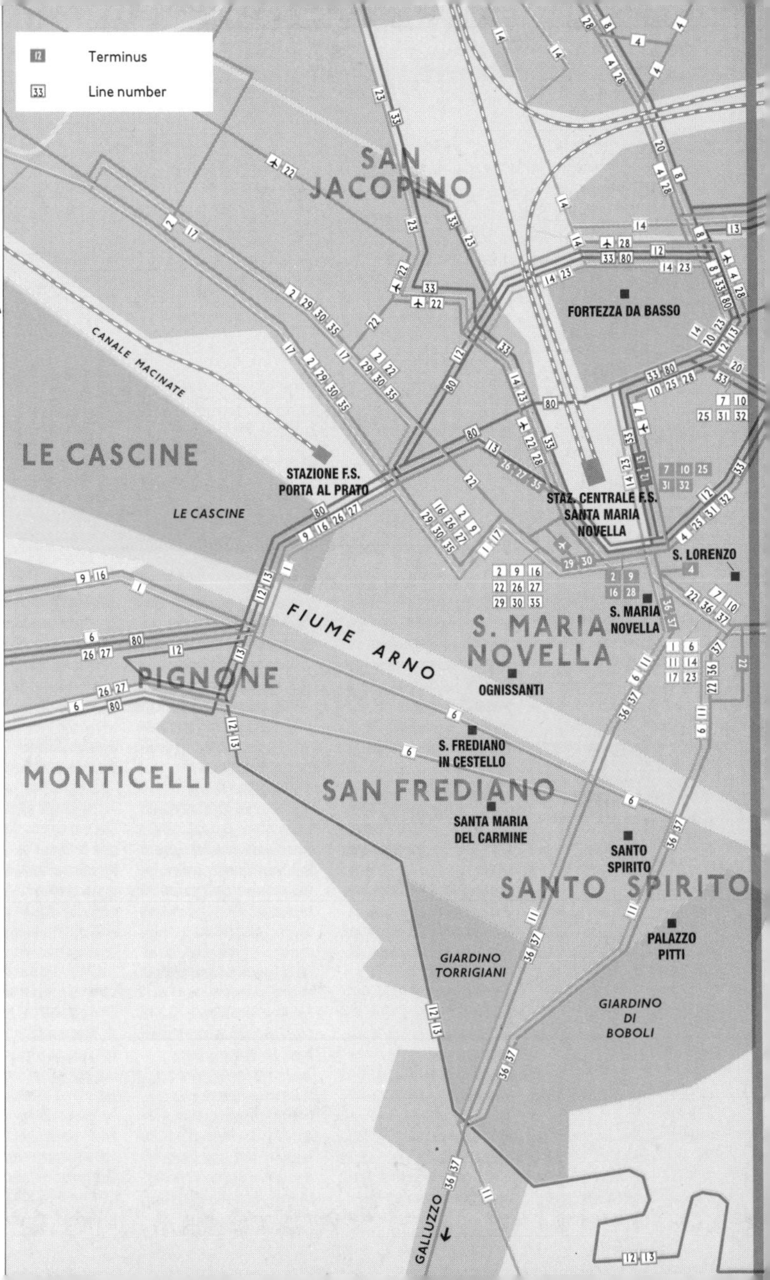

Letters (**A, B, C...**) relate to the matching sections. Letters on their own refer to the spread with the useful addresses. Letters followed by a star (**A★**) refer to the spread with the fold-out map and the places to visit. The number (**1**) refers to the double page **Welcome to Florence!** at the beginning of this guide.

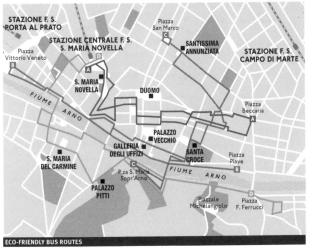

ECO-FRIENDLY BUS ROUTES

Map labels: STAZIONE F. S. PORTA AL PRATO, Piazza Vittorio Veneto, STAZIONE CENTRALE F. S. S. MARIA NOVELLA, Piazza San Marco, SANTISSIMA ANNUNZIATA, STAZIONE F. S. CAMPO DI MARTE, S. MARIA NOVELLA, DUOMO, Piazza Beccaria, FIUME ARNO, PALAZZO VECCHIO, GALLERIA DEGLI UFFIZI, SANTA CROCE, Piazza Piave, S. MARIA DEL CARMINE, P.za S. Maria Sopr'Arno, FIUME ARNO, PALAZZO PITTI, Piazzale Michelangiolo, Piazza F. Ferrucci

rooms have double-glazing. 83–109 €.

Villa Agape (**F** D4)
→ *Via Torre del Gallo 8/10*
Tel. 055 22 00 44/233 70 12
Take bus 12 or 13 then bus 38 to this gorgeous refuge run by nuns, far from the bustle of the city, just above San Miniato. The villa looks out onto a garden full of boxwood trees, cypresses and an olive grove. Free parking. Dinner available. 100 €.

Soggiorno Pergola (**D** B2)
→ *Via della Pergola, 23*
Tel. 055 21 38 86
Cozy, well-equipped studio apartments for long stays, often used by the musicians and actors from the theater opposite. 100 €.

103–130 €

Belletini (**A** A1)
→ *Via de' Conti, 7*
Tel. 055 21 35 61/28 29 80
Peaceful, cozy rooms, a

minute-walk from Michelangelo and San Lorenzo . Both décor and staff are stylish: this contributes to a very pleasant stay. 124–150 €.

Albergo la Scaletta (**E** F2)
→ *Via Guicciardini, 13*
Tel. 055 283 028/214 255
Exceptional location: the terraces on the top floor of this 15th-century hotel afford a view of the Boboli Garden and the rooftops. Each of the exquisitely decorated rooms has its own character. Breakfast included. 125 €.

Pensione Annalena (**E** D3)
→ *Via Romana, 34*
Tel. 055 22 24 02/96 00
Opposite the most unobtrusive entrance to the Boboli Garden, this 16th-century palace with its faded façade, has balconies overlooking the gardens and 22 tasteful rooms. 120–159 €.

130–155 €

Aprile (**B** E3)
→ *Via della Scala, 6*
Tel. 055 216 237
All the beauty of a romantic palace. Every room has its own distinctive style. Some are decorated with frescos. Rooms either have a view of Santa Maria Novella, the garden or the terrace. Special deals when staying two to three days in low season. 130–170 €.

Burchianti (**B** F3)
→ *Via Giglio, 8*
Tel. 055 21 27 96
Sweet dreams come as standard in the frescoed rooms of this stately 16th-century residence, which has recently been given a makeover. 140 €.

Alessandra (**B** F4)
→ *Borgo Santi Apostoli, 17*
Tel. 055 283 438
Rooms with classical décor and fine views over the church square (n° 10), of the Arno river (n° 22 or

n° 5), or simply of the peaceful street. 100–145 €

Casci (**C** B3)
→ *Via Cavour, 13*
Tel. 055 211 686
Friendly, family-owned hotel, between the Duomo and San Marco. Decent rooms overlooking the courtyard or the street (double-glazing). Large breakfast. 90–135 €.

California (**C** B4)
→ *Via Ricasoli, 30*
Tel. 055 28 34 99/27 53
Peace and quiet and all mod cons in red rooms done out in satin, ivory and wood, with marble bathroom. N° 123 has a view of the Duomo. Breakfast (buffet) on the terrace. 90–150 €.

155–190 €

Orto de'Medici (**C** B3)
→ *Via San Gallo, 30*
Tel. 055 48 34 27
This 19th-century residence